We Who Wove with Lotus Thread

We Who Wove with Lotus Thread

Summoning Community in South India

AARTI KAWLRA

With a Foreword by

PRASANNAN PARTHASARATHI

Orient BlackSwan

WE WHO WOVE WITH LOTUS THREAD: SUMMONING COMMUNITY IN SOUTH INDIA

ORIENT BLACKSWAN PRIVATE LIMITED

Registered Office
3-6-752 Himayatnagar, Hyderabad 500 029 (Telangana), India
e-mail: centraloffice@orientblackswan.com

Other Offices
Bengaluru, Bhopal, Chennai, Guwahati,
Hyderabad, Jaipur, Kolkata, Lucknow, Mumbai,
New Delhi, Noida, Patna, Vijayawada

First published 2018

ISBN 978-93-5287-172-8

Maps cartographed by
Sangam Books (An imprint of The Agricultural Development Commercial Credit And Industrial Investment Company Private Limited)

Typeset in
Book Antiqua 10.5/12.6
by Le Studio Graphique, Gurgaon 122 001

Printed in India at
Glorious Printers, Delhi

Published by
Orient Blackswan Private Limited
3-6-752, Himayatnagar, Hyderabad 500 029
e-mail: info@orientblackswan.com

026549
27112017

CONTENTS

FIGURES AND TABLES

Figures

Tables

PUBLIS

on
used in
followin

K. G.
photog
Produc
K. G. Ra
Padma

R. Ven
Saliyar
Padma
Padma
covers
for the
based

Rags
shuttl
Tamil

PUBLISHER'S ACKNOWLEDGEMENTS

For granting permission to reproduce copyrighted material used in this volume, the publisher would like to thank the following individuals and organisations.

K. G. Ramaswami Chettiar's family, for the back cover photograph of members of the Kumbakonam Silk Sari Producers' Association gathered on the sixtieth birthday of K. G. Ramaswami Chettiar, then president of the Tamil Nadu Padma Saliyar Sangam, in Kumbakonam, 1995.

R. Venkatachalapathy, General Secretary, Tamil Nadu Padma Saliyar Sangam, for the following images and photographs: Padma Saliyar Sangam logo with year of registration [1.1]; Padma Saliya Genealogical Tree [4.3]; *Padma Saliya Kural* covers of January 2015 and August 2017 [7.1a and 7.1b]. And, for the updated list of Bhavanarishi shrines in Tamil Nadu, based on which the map [4.5] of the shrines has been drawn.

Rags Raghavan, for the following photographs: hand-thrown shuttle weaving of silk and gold saris [2.1]; a meeting of the Tamil Nadu Padma Saliyar Sangam [4.1]; a Bhavanarishi matham [4.6]; a silk sari showroom [6.1a]—all taken in Kanchipuram.

A. S. Krishnamurthy, Chennai, and Srinivas Raj Bairi, President, Padmashali Officials and Professionals' Association (POPA), Hyderabad, for the image [3.3] of senior members of the Padma Saliyar Sangam on the cover of Telugu newsletter *Padma Jyothi*, 1982.

C. Thirumalai Chettiar, for the image [4.2] of the second (1987) and third (2010) editions of the *Bhavanarishi Puranam* in Tamil.

S. Gopalaswami, for permission to translate the poem '*Nulum Nulum*'.

FOREWORD

The heavy silk saris of Kanchipuram are the height of South Indian tradition. Worn at weddings by brides and guests alike as well as at other festive and fancy occasions, the striking contrast between body and border, the rich *zari* work, and the elaborately designed *pallavs* are immediately recognisable even to the untrained eye.

Given their importance in South India, it is surprising that these saris, and the weavers who make them, have received little scholarly attention. Aarti Kawlra's *We Who Wove with Lotus Thread* is the first comprehensive study and it represents a major contribution to our knowledge of dress, cloth and weaving in South India.

As is often the case with hoary traditions, the Kanchipuram silk sari made its appearance recently. South India has a long and venerable history of hand-spinning and hand-weaving, but in cotton. Even well into the nineteenth century the weavers of Kanchipuram and Arani specialised in cotton cloth, albeit of the most superb fineness. The shift to silk is of more recent origin and this long experience with making the finest cotton cloth in South India may have been a prerequisite for this move.

Kawlra shows that the form of the Kanchipuram sari is also of recent origin, and that Rukminidevi Arundale was a pivotal figure in the making of it. At Kalakshetra, established in 1936 under the aegis of the Theosophical Society which was headquartered in nearby Adyar, Arundale spearheaded a revival of arts and traditions. Under her leadership, the *sadirattam* or solo dance practiced by *devadasis* was remade as *bharatanatyam*, the classical dance of India. Dancers needed saris and it is here that the Kanchipuram sari made a dramatic public appearance. Kawlra writes: 'Rukminidevi's dance costumes on stage evolved over a period of time and included both sewn and draped sari costumes, always made from the bright contrast-bordered silk saris woven at Kalakshetra. Her experiments in sari design were arbitrated by the notion of "timeless appeal" and ultimately established indices of the traditional in the *korvai* silk sari.'

Two of the great traditions of Tamil Nadu—bharatanatyam and the Kanchipuram silk sari—emerged together in the grounds of the Kalakshetra, which was itself established by a band of Europeans and Indians who came together under the banner of Theosophy. Such is the stuff of tradition.

Both of these South Indian traditions went national. Bharatanatyam became the classical dance of independent India. And Kanchipuram saris became the dress of sophisticated elite women across the country. These traditions were then projected around the globe through vehicles such as 'Festivals of India.'

The new tastes for such silk saris and the growing demand for them had to be met and this is where enterprising weavers in Kanchipuram, Arani, Swamimalai, Kumbakonam and other silk weaving centres in Tamil Nadu enter the story. Many of the weavers who wove these saris hailed from the Padma Saliyar community, a Telugu-speaking caste long settled in urban and rural areas of Tamil Nadu. In several fascinating passages Kawlra describes the local and regional organisation of the Padma Saliyars, their great temple ceremonies that help to define the caste such as the *kodiutsavam* or flag hoisting which is celebrated annually at the Kamakshiamman temple in Kanchipuram, and the origin stories of the Padma Saliyars contained in the *Bhavanarishi Puranam*.

While the bulk of the Padma Saliyars focused on the weaving of silk saris, the more entrepreneurial among them began to enter the sari trade. This entailed financing the manufacture of cloth (which meant dealing in raw silk and yarn), stipulating the colours and design motifs, and the marketing of the final product to highly discerning buyers. Kawlra recounts the life histories of three of these enterprising figures.

The most famous of these silk entrepreneurs are Nalli Chinnaswami Chetti and his descendants, who are the proprietors of the famous Nalli Silks franchise. Chinnaswami ventured from his base in Kanchipuram and established the first Nalli shop in 1928, overlooking Panagal Park in the city of Madras, now Chennai. Under the leadership of his grandson, Nalli Kuppuswami Chetti, the business grew enormously. Kuppuswami shrewdly entered into a marriage alliance with the daughter of a medium-sized sari manufacturer in Kumbakonam, which gave Nalli access to the products of the looms of that silk centre.

Today Nalli markets the wares of more than 10,000 weavers scattered across the towns and villages of Tamil Nadu. It now boasts showrooms across India as well as in Singapore, New Jersey and California. The Nalli business acumen is apparent upon entering its great base in Panagal Park. Kawlra writes: 'The salesmanship of the male staff betrays a keen understanding of the colour and design preferences of women patrons. Selected saris are deftly exhibited with patience, unmindful of the number of saris pulled out or the time involved in re-folding them. The entire operation is skillfully orchestrated—there is a particular way in which the sari is spread out to reveal its pattern without losing grip over its original fold and without appearing clumsy whilst draping the sari's ornamental end-piece over the left shoulder for the benefit of the customer.'

Only a small number of Padma Saliyars are entrepreneurs. For the remainder, work at the loom provides not only subsistence but also meaning. Kawlra beautifully reconstructs the organisation of the weaver household and the details of the work that goes into producing a silk sari. The unity of the weaver's body with the weaver's loom is the highlight of this discussion as she argues, in a stunning piece of ethnographic insight, that work, loom and body achieve a 'metonymic unity' in which parts of the loom correspond to parts of the human body.

Time does not stand still, however. Fashions change and competitors are replacing Kanchipuram silks. Technologies change and power looms are displacing handlooms. Young Padma Saliyar men are seeking employment in Chennai and elsewhere in catering, private security, auto manufacturing, and IT. Older weavers in Kanchipuram are cashing in on the inflation in real estate and selling their houses, which had once been the location of production. But for those of a certain generation, weddings will always be associated with Kanchipuram saris. Kawlra has done a brilliant job of unpacking that moment.

PRASANNAN PARTHASARATHI
Professor of History
Boston College, Massachusetts

AUTHOR'S PREFACE AND ACKNOWLEDGEMENTS

The PhD thesis, from which this book has evolved, was a multi-sited ethnographic monograph of a caste group engaged in handloom weaving in Tamil Nadu. During the course of the two decades since it was submitted at the Department of Humanities and Social Sciences of the Indian Institute of Technology, Delhi, I have engaged with diverse conceptual frames that pervade popular and expert representations of handloom weaving. This book explores handloom weaving in the light of the different regimes of value—craft (as opposed to machine) aesthetic, traditional technology, cottage industry and embodied work—that circumscribe its lived reality in south India.

Using the famous Kanchipuram sari as an entry point of research, I have traversed multiple sites of meaning associated with handloom weaving in Tamil Nadu. What is the salience of these saris among urban consumers, private and state-supported retailers, design revivalists, wholesale producers and weavers using different loom techniques? A common adage among weavers implicates the medieval town of

Kanchipuram to represent handloom weaving as a dynamic profession: 'Kanchipuram *ponal kalatti pozhaikalam*' meaning: One can go to Kanchipuram and survive by pressing one's feet (on the loom). Kanchipuram is imagined and valued in this case as a place of self-reliance and sustenance in the face of uncertainties. Kanchipuram also represents the humble beginnings of the Nalli group, among the oldest and largest family-owned retailer of silk wedding saris in Tamil Nadu. And for consumers, designers and producers of silk wedding saris, Kanchipuram is a brand signifying the 'genuine' contrast bordered silk and gold sari.

Community biography rather than the social history of a caste group is the analytical field and scope of my inquiry. I have focused on what community members do and, say they do, as well as on how wider forces of colonialism, nationalism, capitalism, economic development, and class are negotiated as a group in the course of the everyday. My investigations have led me to the intertwining trajectories of the Padma Saliyar caste association and articulations of its members within macro-level discourses and processes. As a hereditary weaving caste even while they seek 'Other Backward Class' status within the Indian state's affirmative action programme; as repositories of 'tradition' riding the wave of cultural nationalism associated with the emergence of *Bharatanatyam* as an Indian classical dance form on the one hand and, Gandhi's swadeshi nationalism on the other; and as prominent players in the growth and development of the silk handloom sari industry in twentieth-century Tamil Nadu.

We Who Wove with Lotus Thread pays tribute to all those who believe that a shared past of having once woven with lotus thread is a matter of community pride in the present. I have met many members of the Padma Saliyar Sangam in Tamil Nadu who live their lives by this maxim. To them I express my deepest gratitude for sparing their time and attention during the different stages of completion of this work.

I am grateful to S. A. Thilakendran who spent many hours sharing information related to the caste association and its members in the Sangam office at V C Garden, First Street, in

Mandaveli, Chennai. I am especially thankful for his efforts in mapping the distribution of Padma Saliyars in Tamil Nadu on the basis of shrines dedicated to their caste deity, Bhavanarishi. In November 2015 the Sangam lost its most dedicated general secretary. For me it was the loss of a teacher whose depth of understanding of life and living I had only just begun to grasp.

The biography of the community could not have been retold without A. S. Krishnamurthy of Korattur in north Chennai, whose accounts of involvement with the Sangam as Telugu interpreter and translator have been simply invaluable. His personal collection of old photographs, commemorative events' souvenirs and out of print caste literature have served as a community archive complementing oral histories of the Sangam. I am extremely grateful to him for his scholarly insights and the unconditional support he has extended to me for over two decades.

R. Venkatachalapathy, the newly appointed general secretary of the Sangam from Trichy, gave me his own copy of the 2010 edition of the *Bhavanarishi Puranam* and unfailingly fulfilled all my requests for information, particularly with regard to updating the map of Bhavanarishi shrines in Tamil Nadu. I am extremely thankful to him for his efforts.

In Kanchipuram, Dr. Sumati Ayyah and Nalli Babu invited me to attend many meetings and ceremonial events at local temples conducted under the aegis of the Sangam's Kanchipuram chapter. I cannot thank them enough for their kindness and keen interest in helping me with my research. Nalli Babu's sudden demise in March 2017 was a shock as he had not only been an active leader of the Sangam but also championed the cause of handloom weavers in Kanchipuram. It was through him that I had had the opportunity to meet and interview a number of silk weavers and merchants who belonged to the Sangam as well as those belonging to other caste groupings, cooperative societies and weavers' associations.

In Kumbakonam, K. G. Ramaswami, his wife Sathyavathidevi and brother late K. G. Rangaswami opened up their home on J. P. Kovil Street to me. I shall be forever indebted to the entire family for their generous hospitality during my stay with them in the initial years of my field work as well as during several other visits later.

In Swamimalai, I cannot forget J. Nathamuni whose sagacity helped me grasp the true significance of the handloom as a body-scale technology and weaving as a communal activity of sustenance. I wish to thank members of his family for welcoming me back to their home years after his demise.

My heartfelt thanks go out to the numerous institutions, individuals, colleagues and friends who have contributed in more ways than they know to this book. I am grateful to Nalli and Kumaran at Panagal Park and Radha Silks in Mylapore, Chennai, for the hours spent in their showrooms and for the information shared with me. Drawing up the genealogies to link the different leading silk families was an academic exercise that first alerted me to the fact that all three belonged to the Padma Saliyar community. Special thanks are due to K. Rajaram of Sundari Silks, T. Nagar, for his generosity in providing me access to their weavers and looms at Thirucherai and Arani, and to his son Shankar for sharing a photograph of their showroom in Chennai.

At the Kalakshetra Foundation in Thiruvanmiyur, Chennai, I thank Sreerenjini for helping me navigate my way around the library and archives and especially for introducing me to Ulaghanathan, the foreman at the Weaving Centre. I am ever so grateful to Leela Samson, alumnus and former director of Kalakshetra, for sharing her graduation photograph at such short notice.

I began revisiting the dissertation under a Fellowship from the Department of Humanities and Social Science at IIT Madras in 2011–2012. My friends and colleagues there, especially Sonika Gupta and Binitha Thampi were pillars of strength, and I thank them for the unconditional support I received. To P. Sukumari, who was a guest faculty at the time, I owe a field trip to Kanchipuram and smooth interviews in Telugu.

At the International Institute of Asian Studies in Leiden, the Netherlands, I experienced a sense of coming home to a wonderfully collegial atmosphere. Here I met many fine scholars, including Ludwig Pesch to whom I owe a big thank you for his comments on Kalakshetra at my presentation. Words are not enough to convey my gratitude to Nira Wickramasinghe, Gwen Bennett, Antonella Diana and Yoshi Kikuchi who helped me see so much beyond myself. And to Michael Herzfeld I pay my respects for combing through the manuscript as an anthropologist and scholar, but most of all as a teacher.

The time spent as a Fellow at the Nehru Memorial Museum and Library, New Delhi, was also very special. I was not only able to complete a first draft of the book but also had the advantage of a great cohort of colleagues. I thank especially Malavika Kasturi, Rashmi Pant, Anshu Malhotra and Mahesh Rangarajan for their inputs and support at different times during my two years at Teenmurti. I cannot thank V. Sujatha enough for her suggestions on the book abstract, which I took very seriously.

I had spent a lot of time at the Madras Institute of Development Studies in the 90s while completing the dissertation. Many points in the book however took shape after conversations with S. Anandhi, M. Vijayabaskar and A. R. Venkatachalapathy. I am extremely grateful for their insights. I also thank Raman Mahadevan for sharing his research material on handlooms in Tamil Nadu with me.

I am ever so appreciative of the support given to me by The School, Krishnamurti Foundation of India and especially Jayashree Nambiar for giving me the space to work in the study above the office at Damodar Gardens.

I am thankful to the many friends who have seen me through the final stages of this work, especially Dr. S. Subbiah for translating the speech by S. D. Devarajan of the Padma Saliyar Sangam's Kanchipuram chapter; Bhamini Narayanan and Ramaa Ramesh for translating portions of K. S. Parthasarathi's biography; V. Sujatha and L. Kannan for translating S. Gopalaswami's poem '*Nulum Nulum*' and for numerous readings of the *Bhavanarishi Puranam* in Tamil back in the 1990s when we were all part of the People's Patriotic Science and Technology (PPST) Group in Chennai; aunty Kokila Ramakrishnan for patiently pouring over all the material in Tamil with me; Meera Srinivasan for digitising all the secondary material I had collected from the Sangam over the years; and Arati Chari for photoshopping the illustration of two pit looms that her office had meticulously drawn for me in the 1990s.

I shall always be indebted to Prasannan Parthasarathi for helping me initiate the book process and, most of all, for reminding me to let go.

This work has taken a long time. But it could not have been earlier either. Gayatri had to grow up enough to be my sounding board and to provide the title of the book; and Dhruv had to learn that a story can be told only when it is *ready* to be told.

This book is dedicated to Manish who has stood by me through all its drafts.

NOTE ON TRANSLITERATION

Diacritical marks have not been used in this script and adjustments to the transliteration system have been employed—*ch* for *c*, *v* or *w* for *v*, and *sh* for *s*—to facilitate pronunciation. Instead of a strict transliteration of Tamil terms, an effort has been made to keep as close as possible to local pronunciation in their spellings. Thus the use of *th* is to indicate the soft *t* as in 'then.' Again, *zh* is employed in Tamil words like *kuzhi* which is nearest to its original pronunciation. Proper nouns, however, appear in their modern English usage. Instead of 'Saaliyar' I have spelt it as 'Saliyar' and instead of 'Bhaavanaa' it is 'Bhavana.' Non-English terms, excluding names, have been italicised in their first appearance, except words that are in common English language usage, for instance, 'sari,' 'guru,' 'rishi.' I have used the new name for Madras city, Chennai, most of the time except when it is in context of its use prior to the change.

ONE

CLAIMS OF COMMUNITY

And caste haunts all assertions of return to a premodern past, all claims about the glories and values of tradition. Caste may be the precipitate of the modern, but it is still the specter of the past[1]

Anthropology's conflation of caste with religion has eclipsed scholarly interest in caste's legitimations and de-legitimations in relation to the explicitly economic and the mundane. Capital's emphasis on private property has equally disavowed strategies of culture in fostering forms of community that sanction and inculcate the production and reproduction of public good.[2] Rather than situating the analysis of caste within a brahminical model of hierarchical ranking or in the radical anti-caste politics of historically subjugated groups, this book is foremost about the 'work' of community in negotiating caste as the basis for claiming equal rights. Community as it unfolds in this book is the fugitive precipitate of individual and collective responses to hegemonic structures and historical contingencies. In attending to narratives and reproductive strategies associated with hand-weaving, my aim is to view community in its dialectical self-becoming, actively re-constituting and re-articulating caste distinction for collective advantage.[3]

We Who Wove attends to claims of silk weaving as hereditary work among the Telugu-speaking Padma Saliyars in Tamil Nadu. There are other groups whose caste-assigned occupation is silk weaving in Tamil Nadu. The Saurashtras, also known as the Pattu-nulkaars, literally 'silk-thread weavers,' are known for their historical pre-eminence in the handloom industry during the colonial period.[4] I have chosen to explore assertions of occupational specialisation among the Padma Saliyars because members of their community were at the helm of regional, national and international trade in silk handloom saris when I began research in the mid-1990s. This period coincided with the formal registration of the Tamil Nadu chapter of their caste association as well as the official entry of the caste title 'Padma Saliyar' into the central list of Other Backward Classes (OBC) category of national-level caste-based state dispensations for affirmative action.[5]

The polarisation of caste along the brahmin-non brahmin axis in the historiography of caste has overshadowed studies of the re-articulation of caste identities among non-radicalised groups with intermediate positions in south India. Caste is recognised as a 'site of collisions' where claims for both the emblems and actual gains of power and privilege are made and contested.[6] Caste consciousness was galvanised during the non-brahmin movement which challenged the longstanding monopoly of brahmins in the use of heredity in the reproduction of caste privilege for economic and social advantages under colonial rule.[7] The colonial juxtaposition of caste with biologically inherited skill had disassociated weavers and other producer groups from the advantages of modern text-based technical education, which had become the preserve of brahmins who were thought to have an aptitude for the 'learned professions.' Caste-based politics fuels grassroots mobilisation and inter-caste clashes, not only to confront longstanding social and ritual oppression but also to defend caste privilege and guarantee secure economic futures vis-à-vis the rising Dalit, the formerly 'untouchable' groups.[8] I am interested in examining collective strategies employed by the Padma Saliyars in upholding silk weaving as a caste-specialisation because identities are constructed within, and not outside the prevailing discourse of caste which is 'a legitimate category of democratic politics' in south India.[9]

The crystallisation of weaving identities via colonial anthropology and census enumerations differentiated and marked some castes as 'weaving castes' on the basis of their 'hereditary' and 'full-time' engagement in weaving, excluding others as 'part-time,' 'new entrants' or 'untouchable' weavers.[10] The fact that weaving had a differentiated base of producers associated with diverse, consumer-specific varieties of cloth is significant to my argument as it illuminates a politics of difference in the assertion of work-based caste identities. The relatively recent appearance of Padma Saliyar individuals in Chennai's cultural public sphere as patrons of upper caste dominated temples and festivals of music and dance indicates the deployment of caste in acquiring cultural capital on the basis of their (past and present) distinction as weavers of auspicious silk cloths. Conceiving caste as a practice of community rather than as an essentialised, enumerated and encumbered object of state technologies of power draws attention to the 'desires for democratisation' that undergird the self-affirmation of weaving as a hereditary occupation among the Padma Saliyars.[11] I am therefore concerned with the multivocal narratives available to subaltern groups in coping with the changing terrain of power and privilege in postcolonial Tamil Nadu.

The narrative of nation (and of capital) did not attract E. V. Ramaswamy Naicker, founder of the 'Self-Respect' movement who sought caste-based reservations or discriminatory privileges on the basis of level of 'backwardness' from the colonial state in Madras.[12] He terminated his active involvement with the Indian National Congress party in 1925 when his demand for proportionate 'communal representation' was rejected in the meeting held at Kanchipuram town amidst large numbers of handloom weavers.[13] In 1937 the launch of the anti-

Hindi agitation by the self-respecters mobilised a spectrum of subaltern subjectivities in support of a reconstituted version of Tamil.[14] By the 1950s however, the radical anti-caste, anti-patriarchal, atheist egalitarianism of the non-brahmin movement had attenuated as an emancipatory agenda for non-brahmin groups.[15] The heterogeneity of groups subsumed under the non-brahmin category (especially those who were not indigenous Tamils like the Padma Saliyars) augured divergent paths to upward mobility and social integration in the emergent nation.

The historiography of handloom weaving in south India has inserted hitherto neglected artisan and agrarian mercantile caste-based groups within regional, national and global histories of industrialisation.[16] The literature stresses the dynamic role played by agrarian-artisan merchants in deploying small amounts of accumulated capital towards cloth manufacture on an 'informal' basis in the early decades of the twentieth century, and points to the regionally distinct forms of expansion of towns and cities in the postcolonial period.[17] This 'alternative view' to the dominant 'de-industrialisation' thesis underscores coping strategies of weaving castes in the face of market adversity—migration, strong social ties, collective bargaining, a capacity to reapply existing skills to new consumer products and the ability to adopt mechanised efficiencies—and recasts individuals and leaders among them as 'agents of innovation.'[18]

The emergence of a mass market for handcrafting skills and new product varieties has been stressed in studies of consumption patterns during the early twentieth century in India. The products in demand were consumer-oriented and responsive to shifts in prevailing attitudes and structures of patronage and preference for artisanal products.[19] In the case of handloom cloth, this dynamic was co-incident with the growth of silk weaving towns like Kanchipuram in Tamil Nadu.[20] Investigating the articulation of caste along spatially distinct levels of production organisation—the city, town and weaving household—builds upon this paradigm of regional growth and collective/individual agency.

The designation of the handloom as an aspect of 'tradition' in reformist and revivalist discourses pronounced weaving as being nationally significant. It offered hereditary weaving castes a fresh ideology for self-representation and political mobilisation on the basis of their work and labour. The invocation of the 'powers of production' of 'producing communities' whose work 'made possible the riches of Indian civilisation' by non-brahmin leaders like P. Theagoraya Chetty, hailing from the Telugu Devanga weaving caste, did offer relatively marginalised weaving groups a fresh impetus for claiming social and political equality in the non-brahmin movement's early years.[21] Anandhi notes that weaving communities did attempt to participate in the movement through 'self-respect' weddings. Moreover, Saliyar (it is not clear whether this reference is to the Telugu or Tamil speaking Saliyars) advertisements of weddings, conferences and resolutions were often found in the pages of *Kudiarasu*, indicating their identity with the movement.[22] By the 1950s however, Dravidian nationalism had given way to caste association politics. The Congress party in Madras saw weavers as an influential political constituency and in 1936 sponsored protest marches across the province on 'Weavers' Day' to highlight the impoverished condition of handloom weavers in the face of competition from mills.[23]

Padma Saliyar leaders had begun to redraft the cause of handloom weavers into wider national agendas in the first half of the twentieth century. Their role as exemplary leaders upholding the interests of their community and the rise of successful Padma Saliyar silk merchants in Tamil Nadu post-independence is testimony to the path a particular non-brahmin caste chose to take. Padma Saliyar individuals played a vital role in handloom weavers' movements against the industrialisation of textile production, and their contributions on the national stage have been seen as shared achievements and valorised in caste association meetings, conferences and publications. Pragada Kotaiah (1915–1995), protégé of Gandhian economist and political leader N. G. Ranga, was not only responsible for mobilising economically stranded weavers into cooperatives but also linked their struggle to weavers nationwide as general secretary of the All India Handloom Weaver's Congress, founded in 1945 under the guidance of Mahatma Gandhi at Nagpur. Kotaiah was elected member of the State Legislative Assembly of the composite state of Madras in 1952 and responsible for the establishment of a separate ministerial portfolio for handlooms in several state governments across the country. During his tenure at Madras, Pragada Kotaiah is known to have made representations to successfully include the Padma Saliyars into the state Backward Classes list, which has subsequently helped to raise educational levels and job opportunities for the caste group.[24]

K. S. Parthasarathi (1910–1990), a Padma Saliyar leader well known as Thozhar (comrade) 'KSP' among communist circles, played a significant role in rallying silk weavers around class interests and drawing them into the cooperative fold.[25] According to his biographer Ramakrishnan,[26] author of *Nesavalar Iyakkathin Vidivelli* (Dawn of the Weaver's Movement) KSP led a three-dimensional war: against poverty; against corruption; against partisan politics. He was disillusioned by the modernist agenda of the Congress party and became an avowed communist after having been arrested in 1942 for staging the *pasi-pattini* or 'hunger and poverty' protests on behalf of silk handloom weavers reeling under the impact of the *pattu kattupadu* or 'silk embargo' in Kanchipuram.[27] In 1945, KSP petitioned to the district textile officer to ameliorate the conditions of production by instituting silk depots in neighbouring towns of Ponneri, Sriperumbudur, Thiruvalluvar and Chingalpattu; by ensuring weavers who owned their looms were accommodated within the cooperative association and by eliminating membership registration charges for new entrants.

By 1955 KSP had set up the first silk handloom weaver's cooperative, the *Kancheepuram Kamatchi Amman Pattu Kaithari Nesavalar Kootturavu Sangam* enrolling 110 weaver members, most of who were Padma Saliyars. In subsequent years his struggle was directed against the power loom and lobbying extensively for protective state policies for handloom products and producers. Despite having lost the Assembly elections in 1962 to political rival C. N. Annadurai in Kanchipuram, KSP retained his leadership role in the labour movement in Tamil Nadu. As the elected leader of the Marxist Community Party of India, KSP was responsible for the spread of the cooperative movement to other parts of Tamil Nadu and continued to wield considerable influence in official circles.[28] His name is synonymous with The Kamakshiamman Silk Weavers Cooperative Society, which is located on a street named after him. When I visited his home in 2015, it had been converted into an office for the Tamil Nadu Handloom Weavers' Federation.

The field of meaning-making comprising community is not limited to its caste basis and includes ideologies of class and craft. What are the entangled narratives framing handloom weaving since colonial times? I am interested in seeing how the Padma Saliyars articulate difference, generate value and claim place-based rights on the basis of their shared patrimony, whilst negotiating colonial and postcolonial constructs like 'weaver caste,' 'member of a handloom weaver's cooperative,' 'craftsman' and 'Backward Class.' More specifically, in this book I focus my attention on how the Padma Saliyars resist (and claim) top-down imaginaries of their identity through the use of heredity and work practice as a ground for difference in setting themselves apart as 'original' producers of cloth and specialists in the cultural value of auspiciousness.

Padma Saliyars posit themselves 'on par' with brahmins to claim difference through their 'thread' and the divinely ordained work of weaving. 'Our thread is different from the thread of the brahmin'; 'They have the Vedas, we have weaving.' Establishing a genealogical link to the holy trinity of the Hindu pantheon through vernacular versions of the Puranas[29] the Padma Saliyars claim a high status among other weaving castes. Their myth of origin recorded in a Tamil translation of the *Bhavanarishi Puranam* pronounces weaving as a celestial benefaction and alludes to their longstanding recognition and status as those who wove with lotus thread. The Padma Saliyars believe that their cosmic lineage is encoded in the title conferred to them by lord Vishnu himself where *padma* refers to the 'lotus' originating from his navel and *saliyar* is derived from the Sanskrit, *shaalika* or weaver. Another version that proclaims their occupational right to weaving in society traces the root of the word *saal* or spider, likening weaving to the dexterous activity of the spider.

The role played by weavers in expanding markets and the growing importance given to them by kings during the height of temple urbanism in the Vijayanagar period (fifteenth to sixteenth centuries), saw economic prosperity and social mobility among weaving communities. South Indian temple inscriptions abound with references to weavers claiming and contesting public honours through various temple donations made by them.[30] The practice of adding a suffix to the caste name *saliya chetti* or to the item of trade *chilai chetti* or cloth merchant suggests that weavers did indeed have a significant economic presence during that period.[31] The presence of Padma Saliyars in medieval urban centres like Kanchipuram and Thanjavur and their continued links with temples in these areas even today is strongly suggestive of their earlier status as artisans in the region and is resonated in their self-representation in the present.

Historiography of the colonial period illuminates collective agency among weavers with numerous references to caste groupings as a vital source of weaver consciousness and solidarity in south India. Predicated upon kin and supra-local affinal links forged via endogamy, shared identities were articulated through collective donations and rights at important regional temples since the medieval period. In the modern period caste was reiterated in the 'natural' enlistment of specific 'weaving castes' into textile mills and weaving factories as legitimate heirs to weaving.[32] Some castes were labelled 'innovative' on account of the techno-entrepreneurial spirit demonstrated by leaders among them, and were special targets of reformist initiatives undertaken by the Madras Government.[33]

The point is that histories of weaver castes like the Saurashtras of Madurai and Padmasalis of Sholapur reveal the explicit reassertion of collective bodies such as caste associations that mitigated sharp internal differences among groups experiencing changed economic profiles and social circumstances. Roy uses the term 'community' to suggest 'a group that communicates internally with relative ease' but wherein 'inequality and hierarchy were often built into collective activity, and individual agency and collective agency were indistinct.' In this book I make a case for the re-articulation of work identities through caste-based relations in Tamil Nadu. Indeed as Dirks has argued, caste in its modern avatar is 'a reminder that all claims about community are claims about privilege, participation, and exclusion.'[34]

The contemporary Padma Saliyar assertion of privilege as weavers of silk cloth for the gods is resonated in the historiography of hereditary 'weaver castes' who are known to have consistently attempted to surpass their subaltern status—in the medieval period of heterodox sectarian movements in south India weavers are said to have parlayed social and ritual privileges such as that of donating the temple flag and being publically recognised at the *kodi utsavam* or flag festival in regional temples; in the transition to the colonial economy, weavers had substantial bargaining powers vis-à-vis merchants[35]; in the late colonial period they were able to resist 'peasantisation' and find fresh means of employment in the handloom industry through migration[36]; in the first half of the twentieth century weavers are known to have succeeded in building political and economic constituencies via the cooperative movement; and in the post-independence period, through the re-articulation of caste as cultural (craft) heritage amidst the Indian state's enactment of a developmentalist agenda for handloom weaving; and in the late appearance of the Padma Saliyars among the ranks of the middle and upper middle classes in Tamil Nadu.

The Padma Saliyars are unequivocal that the Telugu language, their lineage traced to their mythic ancestor and deity Bhavanarishi attributed to the *Markandeya Purana*[37] and the fact that they once wove lotus thread cloths for the gods differentiates them from other 'weaving castes' in south India. In 1971, based on the recommendations of the Sattanathan committee for the First Backward Class commission of Tamil Nadu,[38] Padma Saliyar representatives had refused to be subsumed under the generic title Saliyar.[39] In 1987, at a meeting of the All India Padma Saliyar Association in Hyderabad in the then state of Andhra Pradesh, the issue was re-opened by representatives of the Tamil-speaking Saliyar community, numerous in and around the Srivilliputhur, Rajapalayam and Thirunelveli region of Tamil Nadu. They proposed the merging together of their community with the Padma Saliyars under the generic title Saliyar. Padma Saliyar leaders agreed to the suggestion on the grounds that the Saliyars accept Telugu as their mother tongue and Bhavanarishi as their ancestral deity. According to an informant who attended this meeting, the matter remained unresolved as the Saliyars could not comply with these conditions. For the Padma Saliyars, weaving alone does not confer privilege as 'even a neighbour can learn to weave over a period of time' and therefore must be claimed through lineage, language and religion.

The Padma Saliyars are explicit in their declaration of distinctiveness from other weaving groups and in the words of S. A. Thilakendran, the late general secretary of the Tamil Nadu Padma Saliyar association in Chennai, 'wherever there is a Bhavanarishi shrine, you will find members of our community residing in the vicinity.' Recounting his search for a street named 'Padma Saliyar *pettai*' in Kanchipuram to meet with prospective affines in the mid-1990s, a renowned scholar based in Chennai shared with amusement that even though the sign on the street read 'Saliyar *pettai*' the prospective groom's family maintained that they resided on '*Padma* Saliyar *pettai*' and insisted on guiding them to their home accordingly.

Summoning a particular version of the past possessed, upheld and stabilised from within the dialectic of multiple veracities, I propose, is implicated in the work of community as it guards against, in the words of Eric Wolf, 'other possibilities that may threaten truth, fruitfulness or beauty.'[40] So that defence of caste privilege becomes an act of socio-economic mobility and political presence in-this-world whilst also assuring karmic redemption beyond. Viewing the discursive practice of community as a legitimate focus in the historiography and ethnography of artisans, in *We Who Wove* I draw together seemingly unrelated strands—myth, speculative history and daily practice of weaving, worship and social reproduction—as the 'work' of community. I am less concerned with the overall history of the Padma Saliyar caste association and more with the signposts of its constitution, revival and evolution that shed light on the work of community-for-itself by examining biographies of Padma Saliyar leaders and through an inquiry into their conceptions of self-identity and work practices for claiming occupational merit in the past and self-respect in the present.

The speech of a weaving labour activist, delivered at a commemorative function held under the auspices of the Kanchipuram chapter of the Tamil Nadu Padma Saliyar Sangam masterfully invokes myth, ritual, caste, history, place and politics in mobilising caste-based economic constituencies:

> During the rule of Uttama Cholan and the Pallavas, Telugu-speaking Padma Saliyars from Srisailam were brought to Kanchipuram to produce beautiful textiles for the king and his family. Records of administration and official correspondence of the Baramahal district from the colonial period (*The Baramahal Records published from 1907 onwards*) document the existence of a royal edict from that period that conferred the Padma Saliyars residing in and around Kanchipuram the right to weave silk cloths for the royal household and temples and to hoist the flag bearing the tiger at special temple festivals.
>
> Among the Padma Saliyars settled in Kanchipuram are those who bore the name *Vellaichilaikarars*, literally 'those who donned (or wove) white cloth.' This was the Pandari clan whose leader or *Peddanakkarar* had the right to hoist the community's flag during Brahmotsavam festivals at the Ekambaranathar temple, Kamatchi Amman temple, Kumarakottam temple and Yodatthakari Perumal temples in Kanchipuram. His other duties were to collect one rupee for every loom during weddings and on festivals. The fund thus created was used for the welfare of the community.

> This association, originally named the *Kanchipuram Padma Saliyar Pandariyar Vakaiyara Dharma Paripalana Stapana Sangam*, has been carrying out its functions for the last forty years. It participates at temple flag hoisting festivals and provides free food during the festivals of *Adi Krithigai* and *padisevai* at the Thiruthani temple. It supplies free books and note books to school children. It has helped the Thirthani *chathiram* [community hall] to earn a regular income on behalf of the Padma Saliyars in the district.
>
> Many in the community have helped the sangam to continue and fulfill its goals. There is lot more to be done in the times to come under the current leadership.... The Pandari clan was the recipient of a royal bequest of a piece of land near the Ekambaranathar temple for promoting a flower garden. Efforts are being made to construct a wedding hall on the plot owned by the community on Raja Street and an administrative building for the sangam on the plot owned by the community on Perumal Naidu Street. These projects require larger funding and I am sure members of the community will strive to reach this goal quickly.[41]

The cultural and the economic are not distinct in the 'work' of community and, as this speech demonstrates, are predicated upon the active supplication of the past and its conflation as artisanal identity in the present, for individual and collective gains in the future. Work, as existing capability and future aspiration, is the means by which the personal and the commensal of community life become pervaded by the instrumental, and equally how the community's economic and political arenas become infused by the symbolic. No wonder then that supra-local networks of production, mythic ancestry, technical knowledge and skill, the household as an arena of shared labour, specialised products like cloths for the gods, emerge as 'enunciative strategies' articulating work-based difference among the Padma Saliyars.[42]

Developmentalist approaches have situated 'reform,' 'revival' and 'democratisation' within essentialised stereotypes of community as 'traditional,' 'self-contained' and sedenterised within the frame of village, caste and craft since colonial times.[43]

Such a lens has marked artisanal producers as being out of sync with progress and change. The continued representation of community as the site of a timeless sphere of culture, local knowledge and subsistence economy in development rhetoric has only served to deepen the modernist denial of ongoing constructions of community together with its role in social, political and economic constituency building among subaltern groups.[44]

My objective is to observe *processes* of the production of place, people, objects and relations, rather than *a* place, people, object or relation. In that respect I have sought to re-conceive the ethnographic record on Padma Saliyar engagement in silk handloom sari production in Tamil Nadu over an extended period of time. Instead of viewing artisan groups as repositories of 'local' wisdom, I focus on articulations of community as a 'complex co-production ... by organic intellectuals, administrators, linguists, missionaries and ethnologists ...' made legible through quotidian practices of work, belief and ritual, re-affirmed under unstable social, economic, political and ecological contingencies.[45] And sites of sociality—objects, body, household, street, village, town, region and nation—according to this lens, become comprehensible as substantive relations, variously realised within a matrix of asymmetric domains of action and meaning.

When I began field work in 1994, some of the largest silk businesses in Tamil Nadu—Nalli, Kumaran and Raasi, in Chennai—belonged to Padma Saliyar individuals with a vast kin and affinal network in silk weaving towns like Kanchipuram, Kumbakonam and Swamimalai. From the processing of raw silk yarn to its weaving, stocking and final sales, Padma Saliyars were very visible in the regional production network of silk saris. Members of the community were involved at every level of production and distribution of saris—from retail in big cities, to wholesale production in smaller towns and household-based weaving in villages. Leadership, through professional competence and a common work ethic, is visible at every level of production of silk saris among the Padma Saliyars in Tamil Nadu—at the macro level of retail in big cities, the middle level of production in market towns and at the micro level of the weaving household.

Rather than map the incidence of caste-wise businesses and weaving households with centres of silk weaving in Tamil Nadu to claim or disclaim pre-eminence, I focus on moments of coincidence between the waxing assertion of community and the rise of silk handloom leadership in Tamil Nadu. The decade of the 1990s marked a peak in the reputation and role of the *nattanmaikaran* or community head played by Nathamuni in Swamimalai; the public recognition of K. G. Rangaswami as a leading silk producer in Kumbakonam; and the emergence of Nalli Kuppuswami as a patron of the fine arts in Chennai.

I am interested in Padma Saliyar affirmations of weaving as a shared activity across diverse domains. In temple festivals, in household beliefs and rituals, ceremonies (these could pertain to philanthropy, worship, life-cycle) and in periodic meetings conducted under the auspices of the various district, state and all-India level associations, particularly the Tamil Nadu Padma Saliyar Sangam. Handloom weaving is the primary focus of collective petitions for positive discrimination, subsidies and place-based rights as 'original' weavers of the Kanchipuram sari to the state and central governments.[46] Ethical work practice is the common theme in biographies, speeches, articles, books and websites associated with Padma Saliyar leaders and

Fig. 1.1: Logo of the caste association indicating its year of registration, 1994. The text in the outer circle reads 'Tamil Nadu Padma Saliyar Sangam, Chennai' with a yellow flag bearing the caste symbol of the tiger. The logo featured on the website mast head of the association's monthly magazine, *Padma Saliyar Kural*, until 2016.

Source: http://padmasaliyarkural.com/ Courtesy, R. Venkatachalapathy, General Secretary of the Tamil Nadu Padma Saliyar Sangam, Chennai.

in particular the monthly community magazine, *Padma Saliyar Kural*, or 'Voice of the Padma Saliyars.' I read Padma Saliyar self-representations in these spheres as articulations of community in all its myriad stratagems, variously commingling the past with the present but not limited by it.

My association with the Tamil Nadu Padma Saliyar Sangam began in 1994, which was also the year in which it was officially registered although it had already been functioning in a scattered manner at the local level in the districts of Salem, Kanchipuram, Gudiyattam, Kumbakonam, Tiruchirappalli and many other weaving centres. The Sangam has submitted numerous petitions for gaining entry into the Most Backward Classes (MBC) category whose quota was carved out from the earlier reservation percentage of backward classes implemented in 1989. These have been rejected on various grounds and also contested by other non-brahmin castes such as the Vaniyar dominated PMK (Pattali Makkal Katchi) political party in Tamil Nadu.[47]

The caste association's links have taken me from Chennai (then Madras) to Kanchipuram, Kumbakonam and to Swamimalai where I was able to collect genealogies of key community leaders engaged in silk sari weaving in Tamil Nadu (see Fig. 1.2).

We Who Wove is a testimony of the materialisation of community jostling amidst competing and often conflicting local, regional and national commitments in the twentieth century. I see community as a contested field of meaning-making intertwined in the economic as much as the cultural and political. Such an approach confounds the normatively determined, discrete spaces of identity—class, caste, religion and civil society—and attends instead to the *claims* of a group in the shared pursuit of value (both instrumental and expressive) in everyday life. The erasure of collective histories of sustenance since the entrenchment of capitalist political economy necessitates imaginings of what Uberoi (2012) refers to as 'the brighter side of human work, labour and usage.' In this book I therefore privilege mobilities of work rather than the fixity of property in assertions of ownership and identity.[48]

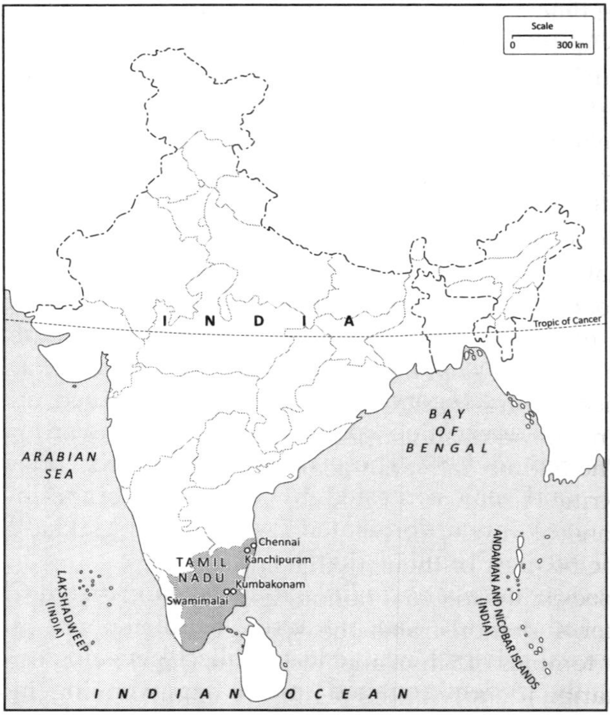

Fig. 1.2: Areas of the author's fieldwork in Tamil Nadu, India.

The chapterisation mirrors a progressive reclamation of work in discursive domains of collective engagement. In chapter 2, I map the twentieth century terrain of discourses on the handloom in the colonial government debates on India's industrial future and the nationalist call for economic self-reliance. Defined in opposition to industrial production, the reconstituted handloom sector enters the domain of culture through the idiom of caste and a renewed patronage for craft. The nationalisation of the *sadir*, a ritualised temple dance, and re-aesthetisation of the contrast-bordered silk sari as the costume of the *bharatanatyam* dancer at Kalakshetra in Madras initiates a discourse of design of the sari, unleashing new opportunities and markets for handloom weavers and producers among the rising middle classes.

In chapter 3, I establish leadership or proven mastery in one's specific area of work as an organising principle in the production of silk saris. Three biographies from three discrete spatial domains of production – the micro level of the weaving household and street, the middle level of wholesale production in towns and the macro level of retail in the city – illuminate mobilities of silk weaving in twentieth-century south India. Public honour within a growing constituency of caste fellows mediated by the caste association is central to the recognition of a leader in Padma Saliyar handloom publics and forms the basis for the sustenance of a dynamic model of distributed production. Cooperative conflicts undergird production alliances along horizontal and vertical lines and take place within supra-kin and supra-local networks of community.

The Padma Saliyars trace their lineage to the high gods of Sanskritic Hinduism – Brahma, Vishnu and Shiva – in various versions of myths of origin which legitimise weaving as a cosmic bequest of their mythic ancestor Bhavanarishi. Rather than see claims to ritual honour as a process of sanskritisation, chapter 4 demonstrates the spatialisation of community in major temples of Shiva and Vishnu in Tamil Nadu to establish a sectarian identity in the region. Worship of caste and family deities in street level shrines and privileging of the loom during life-cycle ceremonies in the household further spatialises community to establish weaving as a distinctive identity in chapter 4.

Countering the ideology of the technical as an 'objective force' external to human comprehension and agency in chapter 5, I examine the weaving household and the centrality of the loom within it as an arena of reproduction and transmission. The interrelatedness of the sacred and the mundane in Padma Saliyar conceptions of work emerges through a reconsideration of the 'common sense' of everyday weaving activities. Goals of consumption, nourishment and sustenance underpin the correlation between work, loom and the body in the household and disavow the subordination of human labour to the universalising ontology of 'machinofacture' and spatialisation of production in the factory system.[49]

Chapter 6 focuses on the discourse of value surrounding the production and exchange of wedding saris in Tamil Nadu. I inquire into the colonial mapping of products within a place-based typology of craft privileging the contrast-bordered *korvai* sari as 'traditional' design. The post-independence fixing of Kanchipuram as a place of origin is an opportunity for authenticating Padma Saliyar self-representations as 'original' producers of the Kanchipuram sari. The conscious enunciation of weaving as the pursuit of auspiciousness in daily life unites them to the consumers of their products in a framework of shared values and substantiates their reputation as specialists in wedding saris.

In the brief closing chapter, I take the opportunity to reflect on the findings of my research whilst taking cognisance of the time elapsed since I first entered the field in 1994. Inserting artisans within histories of capital and labour has underscored their precarious position but privileged the developmentalist state and its economy.[50] Equally, the national and global discourse of heritage has valorised artisanship but continues to deny coevalness to artisans and the products of their work.[51] How does one attend to the subjectivities of work in the context of shifts in raw material supply, markets, consumption patterns, production organisation and technology innovations in handloom weaving since the late colonial period? Reconsidering caste in the polysemous juxtapositions of work, identity and value illuminates the discursive constitution of a social/public life from below. *We Who Wove* is an inquiry into the consciousness of caste as the articulation of subalternity confronting alternative forms of productive organisation in capitalist modernity.

ENDNOTES

1. Dirks 2001:18.
2. Capital and community have been antithetical in Western capitalist modernity. The use of the phrase 'social capital' reflects capital's inadequacy in explicating cases of value generation for the common good (Chatterjee 1998).

3. I am interested in the dynamics of culture and identity, especially in their relations to wider forces of power and economics following the work of Eric Wolf (1982; 1984).

4. Roy 1997; migrations of the Padma Saliyars (tenth–twelfth century) and the Saurashtras (seventeenth century) into present day Tamil Nadu are believed to have strengthened the handloom industry (Haynes and Roy 1999).

5. The Padma Saliyars are listed as distinct from the Saliyar, Pattusaliyar, Pattariya and Adhaviyar, but are placed together with them in entry No. 131 in the central list of OBCs, dated 10 September 1993, of the National Commission for Backward Classes.

6. Dirks 2001.

7. Geetha and Rajadurai 1998; Irschick 1969; Pandian 1993; 1994; 1995; 1996.

8. Harriss 2015.

9. Pandian has shown how Indian upper caste modernity's universalist rhetoric of 'common good' denies an inclusive public sphere as it 'proscribes and stigmatises the language of caste' and 'most often forces the subordinated castes into silence and self-hate' Pandian (2002: 1738).

10. See Miryam 2014 for the case of lower caste Pariahs or Malas engaged in plain cotton weaving from being officially recognised as weavers in colonial records.

11. Chatterjee 1989.

12. Like B. R. Ambedkar, E. V. Ramaswamy sought to 'recover a space for the language of caste in the colonial public sphere' (Pandian 2002: 1737).

13. Pandian 1993.

14. Pandian 1996.

15. Barnett 1975.

16. Baker 1984; Haynes 1985; Roy 1993; Specker 1989; Yanagisawa 1993.

17. See Haynes 2013 on how the expansion of small-scale, informal textile production contributed to rapid urbanisation in western India; Chari (2004) for the rise of the 'knit city' Tiruppur from agrarian (dominant caste) capital in Tamil Nadu and De Neve (2005) for his study of occupational shifts and upward mobility associated with the rise of small-scale textile industries in the towns of Bhavani and Kumarapalayam in Tamil Nadu.

18. Roy 2000; 2007.

19. See the edited volume on history of consumption in South Asia by Haynes et. al (2010).

20. Benaras in UP and Surat in Gujarat were the other two towns that saw this growth according to Roy (2010).

21. Geetha and Rajadurai 1998:135–7.

22. Anandhi 1991: 29. This latter piece of information is based on personal communication.

23. Frasca 1975: 1119–20.

24. Members of the caste association in Chennai recall that Kotaiah was prompted to pursue the matter when a Padma Saliyar youth, having secured a seat in an engineering college at Kakinada, was asked to produce a caste certificate and denied admission on account of the absence of the Padma Saliyars in the Backwards classes list.

25. Arterburn 1982.

26. The weaver's movement in the title and KSP's biography are coterminous for the author. The book is a biography of K. S. Parthasarathi in Tamil, a copy of which I found at the CPI(M) library in Chennai. I am grateful to Bhamini Narayanan and Ramaa Ramesh for the translation of this text.

27. This was due to the shortage of silk yarn and other fine count yarns including artificial silk and mercerised yarn consequent to the Japanese participation in the War (Yanagisawa 1993).

28. In 1982, the Tamil Nadu State Government under then chief minister M. G. Ramachandran was prompt to eliminate the 2 per cent tax on silk handloom products on KSP's behest (Ramakrishan 2001).

29. Caste-puranas deal with the position of a particular caste within the structural order of medieval Hinduism and are said to have been written relatively recently (AD 1200–1700). Texts pertaining to the mythic origins of endogamous caste groups are available for the regions of Gujarat, Maharashtra, Tamil Nadu and Bengal (Das 1982:10–11).

30. Appadurai 1974; Mines 1984; Frasca 1975; Ramaswamy 1985b; Stein 1980.

31. Appadurai 1974; Ramaswamy 1985a: 30–32; Stein 1980: 250.

32. See Haynes and Roy 1999; Miryam 2014. The recent unpublished study by Subramanian on the association of IT with brahmin identity is an example of the ongoing conflation of caste with work and reinforces the colonial subordination and selective 'entexualisation' of local realities in the idiom of caste (Raheja 1996).

33. Roy 2002: 527–8.

34. Dirks 2001: 17.

35. Parthasarathi 2001.

36. Haynes and Roy 1999.

37. Markandeya was a devotee of both Shiva and Vishnu, and this body of Puranic literature holds a unique position as the sacred and secular text of both *shaiva* and *vaishnava* sects of Hinduism.

38. Radhakrishnan 1990.

39. Arterburn 1982: 47.

40. Wolf 1990: 593.

41. I am grateful to Dr. S. Subbiah of the Madras University for a translation of this speech from Tamil, delivered by S. D. Devarajan on 31 December 2012 at the unveiling ceremony of the plaque at the newly built *chathiram* or community hall at Thiruthani town near Kanchipuram.

42. 'Difference' as Hall (2000) suggests becomes a negotiable process rather than a discrete category.

43. Mosse 2006; Sinha 2008; Walker 2009. Citizenship in the colonial imaginary was marked by the privileging of 'sedentarization' over peripatetic forms of social and economic life (Irschick 1994: 191).

44. See for instance Nancy Fraser's formulation of subaltern publics 'where members of subordinated social groups invent and circulate counter discourses, which in turn permit them to formulate oppositional interpretations of their identities, interests, and needs ...' (Fraser 1990: 67). For India, Pandian has discussed how caste becomes a legitimate category, articulating a politics of difference with a guaranteed subaltern public, in modern democratic politics (Pandian 2002).

45. Appadurai 1995: 210.

46. Positive discrimination in Tamil Nadu guarantees 69 per cent of government jobs and educational entitlements to designated 'backward classes' on a preferential basis. The list is a dynamic one and is altered following periodic reviews of changes in social, educational and economic factors.

47. In 1987, the Tamil Nadu Government conceded to the demands of the representatives of the Vanniyar caste for allotting 20 per cent out of the total 50 per cent backward caste reservation for the 'most backward' groups.

48. It is in sharp contrast to the logic of capital, which demands the ownership of private property through the fixing of investments in land or other immovable assets or what David Harvey (2001) has called the 'spatial fix.'

49. This nineteenth-century discourse reconceived the 'factory understood not as a center for the circulation of grain but rather a center for the mechanized production of commodities' (Zimmerman 1997: 7).

50. Ciotti 2007; De Neve 2005; DeNicola 2004; Ganguly-Scrace 2001; Herzfeld 2004; Knorringa 1999; Liebl and Roy 2003; Mamidipudi et.al 2012; Scrase 2003; Subramanian 2009; Wilkinson-Weber 2004, for instance, have engaged with the precariousness of artisanal production.

51. See for example the work of Bundgaard 1999; Maskeill 1999; McGowan 2009; Mohsini 2011 and Venkatesan 2009 on the expropriation of artisans in the discourse of national heritage.

TWO

REFORM AND REVIVAL
Making of a Handloom Tradition

In the first half of the twentieth century an upsurge in demand for higher-valued hand-woven silk cloths took place despite anti-colonial exhortations against fine count mill-made and silk yarns. Gandhi's insistence on hand spinning as an icon of resistance to British rule aimed to bring conscious political practice into people's everyday lives. Gandhi's political agenda was to illuminate the systemic exploitation under capitalist modernity through *khadi*[1] or hand-spun and hand-woven cotton cloth. His strategy was to use the spinning wheel as a polysemic tool to articulate the systemic dominance of structures responsible for the state of economic and moral degeneration in the world. In his words 'the movement of the spinning-wheel is an organized attempt to displace machinery from that state of exclusiveness and exploitation ....'[2]

In his address to representatives of the Saurashtra-led handloom industry in Madura faced with acute scarcity of fine count yarns, Gandhi insisted that spinning rather than handloom weaving was his chosen liberative practice:

> You ask me to encourage hand-weaving even through foreign yarn or mill-made yarn inasmuch as ... it is not possible today to find hand-spun yarn of the fineness you require and in the quantity you require. Now I shall tell you, as a fellow weaver, why I cannot possibly endorse your recommendation.... What has befallen the industry of spinning will most decidedly befall the industry of hand-weaving also if the weaver will not take a leaf out of my book.... If you will study the history of the hand-weaving movement in India you will discover that at the present moment several thousands of weavers have simply been obliged to abandon their trade. Weavers, all of your own trade, Saurashtras, are today working in Bombay as scavengers. Weavers in the Punjab are some of them hired soldiers and some of them have taken to the butcher's trade....[3]

Gandhi disapproved of the use of silk among upper caste Tamil women which he found to be ostentatious. 'They must revert to the original simplicity, and certainly God will be better pleased with those who wear the spotless *khadi* sari as a symbol of inner purity than those who are gaudily dressed.'[4] The cultural preference for silk handloom saris among upper castes in Madras was therefore a matter of concern for Gandhian nationalists advocating non-violence, self-reliance and simplicity through the production and consumption of khadi cloth.

Weaving and wearing silk negated the Gandhian commitment to the daily performance of *satyagraha* or the individual and collective 'disciplinary quest for truth' for emancipation from colonial rule. Gandhian nationalism publically denounced the customary predilection for sumptuous silk cloths among the higher classes in Madras. Congress party chief minister C. Rajagopalachari echoed these sentiments in a speech in Madras:

> How I wish it were possible that some of my dear sisters of Tamil land could go to Assam and see the simple and diligent daughters of that beautiful country at their family looms. The time that highborn ladies spend in laboriously picking and choosing from the silks exhibited in the

> bazaar, their sisters in Assam spend in plying the shuttle and making garments for themselves and their children.[5]

His anxiety about sericulture published in *Young India,* 19 October 1922, was also explicit: 'Few ladies know what cruelty is involved in the beautiful silks they love to wear.... Yet, high-caste South Indian ladies ... revel in the use of silks and spend so much money over them....'[6]

Handloom weaving in south India, nevertheless, was to take a completely different trajectory from the one envisioned by advocates of khadi. The growth of the sericulture industry in south India marked an alternative route for many groups of handloom weavers across the Madras Presidency. The considerable expansion of acreage under mulberry cultivation coincident to the demand for parachutes during World War II led to the emergence of south Karnataka and the contiguous districts of Tamil Nadu and Andhra Pradesh as the leading silk producers in the country and contributed to the revitalisation of the handloom industry in the states.[7] In what follows, I investigate how the defence of the handloom was orchestrated in the hands of reformists and revivalists through the valorisation of silk weaving as an aspect of 'tradition.'

The discourse of tradition encompassing handloom production in India has its roots in nineteenth-century ideas on the stages of social and technological evolution that drew upon Europe's own medieval and pre-industrial past in the transition from feudalism to capitalism. Subjects of empire were accordingly ranked in terms of their 'stage in human development' categorising caste as a bounded cultural configuration articulating a non-modern life-world. Similarly, techno-economic backwardness was encapsulated in the ideology of craft predicated upon a politics of difference buttressed by the orientalisation of handmade products, skills, technologies and associated customs. Capitalist expansion and imperial power fueled a 'traditionalisation'[8] of the colonies so that by the twentieth century caste and craft not only stood for India as a whole but also constituted its 'traditional' core in contrast to Britain's own modernisation.[9]

The colonial constitution of India as tradition-bound and unchanging through caste and craft stabilised an imperial vision and apparatus of power. From the late nineteenth century onwards colonial ethnographers were alerting British officials to the existence of 'age-old institutions through which "traditional" caste elders resolved disputes about both trade and domestic morality' among artisan castes in the south.[10] Yet it was a brahminical version of caste, with its emphasis on ritual pollution, patriarchy and characterisation of the household as a private space upholding religious ideals and biological reproduction that determined colonial perceptions of occupational specialisation. Census enumerations reductively categorised similar but discrete endogamous groups into administrative units of patronage or proscription[11] according to a pan-Indian caste hierarchy, ranking literary ability above manual prowess.[12] Work in colonial discourse was naturalised as aptitude through essentialised notions of caste, yielding occupational groupings such as 'weaving caste.'[13] This suturing of a craft skill with hereditary caste confined work identities to the realm of an ahistoricised tradition in discourses of reform and revival and paved the way for the official denial of political, economic and technological agency among weavers and other artisan groups.

Through an examination of the arguments of those advocating the industrial reform of existing handloom organisation and technology, and those urging its cultural revival by stressing the traditional appeal of its products, I now draw attention to the colonial marginalisation of weavers in the making of a 'handloom tradition.'

Colonial policies on handloom production drew upon concepts derived from European textile historiography to interpret the situation in India. Two analogies, of the medieval guild and the 'putting out' system of handicraft manufacture described by Marx, were commonly employed in characterisations of handloom production in south India. Work specialisation and transmission of knowledge via endogamous caste groups was reminiscent of guilds because caste membership and knowledge transmission was both closed and restricted. Guilds were characterised by a centralisation of production and trade under a single 'master' who, although not bound by hereditary considerations in the selection of his apprentices, nevertheless specialised in the teaching of a particular craft to a fixed number of apprentices and journeymen in an urban context.[14] Colonial records of the Madras Presidency validate the Pattu-nulkaars (also called Saurashtras), Padma Sales and Pattusales, Devangas, Kaikolars and Seniyars residing in and around market and temple towns as the known 'weaving castes.' The designation of certain caste groups as 'specialist' or 'hereditary' weavers in colonial documents reinforced internal differentiations within the weaving populace.[15]

The south Indian situation was likened to the pre-capitalist 'putting-out' system because of the practice of distribution of advances to weaving households by organisers of production.[16] The stratification of the weaving population was attributed to the weaver/merchant who was seen to own and control looms, labour and output. The phrase 'master weaver' draws on this parallel with the guild master and merchant-manufacturer of the putting-out system in handicrafts and evokes an unequal and bounded relationship even today.

Both reformists and revivalists highlighted the exploitative role of the alleged 'middleman,' positing weaving castes as bearers of a handloom tradition in opposition to modern industry. The reformist lobby emphasised the class difference between those who owned the means of production and those who merely possessed their labour or ability to weave. Their solutions included the introduction of the factory, cooperative and labour-saving technological improvements in handloom weaving. The revivalist perspective on the other hand disparaged the standardisation of mill-made cloth in a nationalist defence of the handloom, whose products were seen to embody judgements of taste underscored as traditional. Their interventions involved fixing of design parameters and revitalisation of the market for culturally valued goods along the lines of an aestheticised Indian tradition.[17]

INDUSTRIAL REFORM: SMALL FACTORIES AND COOPERATIVE ORGANISATION

Handlooms were the focus of special state attention in the Madras Presidency, where weavers were not only found in large numbers, but also because of rising rural interests as handwoven cloth began to face fluctuations of the international economy and market competition from mill-made cloth. The government discourse in the post-World War I period, comprising seven volumes of the Industrial Commission Report of 1918, explicitly counselled the Indian state to establish rational, efficient organisations like factories, cooperatives, technical schools and industrial museums to facilitate India's industrial development. By the 1930s,

> the "co-operative" became a panacea which government applied to all internal economic problems .... Such problems were blamed on heinous "middlemen," and some form of co-operative was prescribed as the cure. The poverty of handloom weavers was traced to the role of the master weavers and yarn merchants, and weavers' co-operatives were set up as a replacement.[18]

The rhetoric of handloom reform not only recast existing relations of production as exploitative but was also enmeshed within protracted debates on technical education and industrial development. Among its most visible proponents was engineer Alfred Chatterton (1867–1958), the first Director of Industrial and Technical Enquiries of Madras in 1906, who was categorical about separating schools that prepared native boys for manual work requiring physical stamina (class V) and those that provided training in specific trades (class VII) in order to reconstitute handloom weaving along industrial lines.[19]

In Chatterton's assessment, 'Without much enterprise, unaided by capitalists, incapable of adapting themselves to the changes in their environment, and wedded to their antiquated, hereditary methods of working, the artisans have had no resource but to sell their labour at lower and lower rates....'[20] Enunciating weavers as illiterate but skilled workers plying a useful trade in a language presaging developmentalism also meant the fabrication of solutions for ameliorating the situation in a similar vein. His suggestions therefore involved eliminating the *sowcar* or merchant capitalist, providing capital from outside the existing setup and coalescing all operations—from the processing of yarn to its final weaving under the same roof—through the establishment of small handloom factories managed by 'educated men' who were also technically proficient.[21] Such a measure, according to Chatterton, would also solve the problem of providing suitable employment in industry to many of the educated classes: 'The establishment of hand-loom factories will afford excellent opportunities for educated young men to acquire a knowledge and insight into the principles and methods which must be pursued to enable manufacturing operations to be carried on profitably.'[22]

Chatterton's model of the small weaving factory was in tune with the official stand that handloom weaving would eventually have to give way to larger industrial enterprises, for which weavers needed to be prepared. It was based on his experiment in chrome tanning through small-scale factory-based enterprises. These factories, in his view, were prerequisites to his suggestions on technical improvements. Thus a single handloom factory had a dyeing section, a weaving section, and a commercial section headed by experts hired on monthly salaries. The weavers themselves were intended to come from diverse backgrounds and together submit to a common discipline of the factory. In 1906, the Government of Madras, under the advice of Chatterton, set up the first handloom factory in Salem district. In Kumbakonam and Salem these factories were owned and run by members of weaving castes who were already in a position to deploy resources towards these changes whereas in the coastal districts of the Province, members from non-weaving communities were in-charge.[23] Chatterton's reformist agenda thus undertook to 'free' the 'bonded weaver' from the clutches of the 'master weaver' by placing him instead within a factory system of work and habit.[24]

Ernst B. Havell, who began his career as superintendent of the School of Art in Madras in 1884 and was principal of the School of Art in Calcutta till 1905, opposed Chatterton's propaganda of the factory mode of organisation and sought instead to transform handloom production through cooperativisation. Influenced by the movement for a restoration of the medieval guild heralded by architect A. J. Penty in England, and Ananda Coomaraswamy in India, Havell valued the methods of handicraft production over those obtained in strict factory conditions. Like Chatterton, he believed that the local weaving industry could be revitalised 'by the simple expedient of making arrangements to provide the weavers with raw materials on reasonable terms, advancing them cash at reasonable rates in the slack season, and enabling them to obtain the best market price for their labour—all of which advantages are denied them by the rapacious village money-lender.'[25] Havell differed from Chatterton in that he subscribed to social progress through the notion of 'self-help.' In Havell's opinion imperial policy had ignored the system of apprenticeship in small workshops, which he believed was the foundation of the indigenous industrial system in India.[26]

Enamoured by the model provided by medieval European guilds, Havell believed he could revive this system—glimpses of which he already saw among Indian weaving castes—by instilling the value of cooperation among weavers. What was proposed by Havell, however, was a model provided by Danish dairy cooperatives involving the establishment of centres of organisational control run by weavers themselves. Havell insisted that the actual weaving would continue to be carried out, as in the case of the apprentice system, in small workshops or in weavers' own homes by master weavers and their apprentices. The principle of cooperation, itself based on mutual contract, Havell believed, would also lead to character building—'foresight, industriousness, punctuality, honesty, business-capacity, and the other characteristics of a thriving, hopeful and self-respecting community.'[27]

Instead of a factory owned by an individual owner of capital, Havell proposed a centre managed by a committee or board of directors. This centre would provide good quality yarn and dyes to weavers in fifty or twenty-five 'model weaving villages' depending upon the size of the initial capital deposited there.[28] The disbursement of raw materials at lower than market rates would be done through a technically trained manager located in each of these villages who would assist weavers in advancing credit, selling their finished products and train them in the use of improved weaving techniques and appliances. The board or committee would, in turn, be responsible for the satisfactory conduct of these managers. In a few years this scheme would enable weavers to become self-reliant and independent of the local merchant-middleman.

Ideologically, cooperatives represented an egalitarian ordering of society along socialist lines. In policy, however, the main aim of the colonial government in setting up cooperative organisations was the transition to large-scale industrial enterprise. Providing centralised facilities to weavers such as a regular supply of credit, processed yarn and assured sales through marketing outlets, it was thought, would not only rescue them from impoverishment but also train them in the norms of small-scale industrial enterprise.[29]

The reform lobby with its rhetoric of the merchant as an exploitative middleman encouraged the passing of the Madras Cooperatives Act in 1932, following the Depression in which weavers were greatly affected. Cooperative organisation in Madras formally took shape in 1935 when the Madras Handloom Weaver's Cooperative Society was established with a government subsidy.[30] This was also the time when weavers, influenced by the khadi campaign of the nationalist struggle, became involved in agitations and riots demanding that the government look into their socio-economic condition.[31] The Madras Government thus turned its attention to the economic aspect of the industry, instituting a series of reports between 1930 and 1950 that focused on the labour conditions of the handloom industry.[32] When the Congress came to power under C. Rajagopalachari, the Madras state had already made provisions to protect the handloom with increasing government aid.[33] It was the government's policy to involve individuals from non-weaving (caste) backgrounds to control and manage the affairs of handloom weavers who, in its opinion, lacked business and managerial experience and it continues to guide the functioning of weavers' cooperative societies in Tamil Nadu.[34]

The politicisation of cooperatives made weaving accessible to individuals from non-weaving, particularly agricultural backgrounds that could now earn a livelihood or supplement their incomes without having to fall prey to the vagaries of nature. It effectively divided the handloom weaving population into those who owned both looms and capital for investment in raw materials (the master weavers) and those who were loom-less and could only sell their labour, providing opportunities for weavers to join the handloom labour movement and union organisation via the Communist Party of India. Handloom weaving was by now an officially recognised 'cottage' sector of the textile industry. Its labour population, defined in opposition to the centralised mill sector, was believed to be in urgent need of socio-economic reform. The strategy adopted by the colonial administrators for augmenting productivity to complement the re-organisation of handloom production along industrial lines was now outlined as an 'improvement' of hand-weaving technologies.

TECHNOLOGICAL REFORM: THE FLY-SHUTTLE DEVICE

While Chatterton and Havell were sympathetic to India's technological and artistic heritage respectively, both nevertheless subscribed to the legitimacy of colonial modernity.[35] Both placed great faith in modern science and technology, which they thought could be effectively harnessed to bring about greater rationality and efficiency in the 'traditional' handloom. The impetus to bring to Indian soil the fruits of modern science and industrialism was so strong that the weavers' own knowledge and techniques were seen as the cause of their impoverishment. In fact, for Chatterton, weaving on the traditional pit loom was the reason for the widespread destitution among Indian weavers for 'they spent about half their lives buried in the ground' in damp and dark unhygienic conditions. The practice of using a mixture of cow dung and water over the warp and weaving floor to facilitate uniform shedding in fine weaving was considered by him to be an outright 'unsanitary practice.'[36]

A series of technical monographs, written on the basis of information gathered by district collectors, provided the provincial government adequate assessment of the technological sophistication of local weavers to proceed with their plans to upgrade the handloom industry. Thus began the active propagation of 'improved' technologies in the form of labour and time-saving devices both in the preparation of yarn as well as in the actual weaving of cloth. Reformers were careful not to include the power loom in their technological interventions, which implied an outright rejection of handloom weaving. Increased output of the handloom was directly correlated to the time spent (wasted) by weavers in preparing the yarn. Technological reforms, therefore, concentrated on 'hand-powered' machinery, especially for processing yarn.[37] Weavers were familiarised with these technologies through the setting up of training schools, technical institutes, competitions and aggressive propaganda at their doorstep. I focus specifically on one such 'improvement' in the weaving process—the fly-shuttle device—introduced in Madras largely through the efforts of Alfred Chatterton. The widespread adoption of the flying shuttle in Madras, however, has been attributed to the powerful influence of handloom capitalist P. Theagaraya Chetty whose political involvement with the Justice party made him an ideal spokesperson of reform measures among weavers and entrepreneurs.[38]

As Textile Advisor, Chatterton obtained a huge grant from the government for holding a conference and an 'All-India Weaving Competition' at the School of Arts in Madras in 1908. The competition involved the exhibition of a variety of looms from different parts of the country for a demonstration of their yarn processing and weaving techniques. The looms were judged according to the amount of cloth woven in a given time period. For Chatterton and others the success of the competition lay in the fact that it established the 'superiority of the improved fly-shuttle loom over the country loom' which, when extensively adopted, would enable weavers to compete with machine-made products.[39]

The mechanism of the fly-shuttle and the rationale behind its introduction is based on the principle of reducing the time required for interlacing the two sets of threads—the warp and the weft—that constitute the woven cloth. The invention of Kay's 'flying shuttle' in England in 1733 altered the transmitting mechanism[40] in the weaving operation and was noted for its transformation of relations of production by Marx. Whereas the weaver's body remains the driving force in operating the loom, the shuttle carrying the weft yarn is not hand-thrown. Instead it is fitted in a box attached to a rope which the weaver pulls from overhead and whose pulley action rapidly flings the shuttle to and fro horizontally across the warp. The fitting

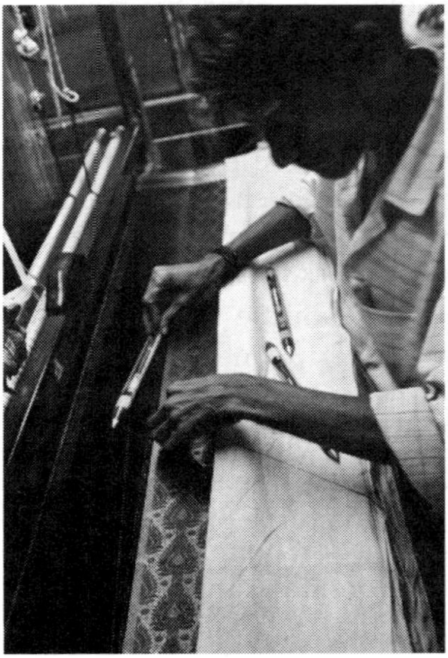

Fig. 2.1: Hand-thrown shuttle weaving of silk and gold saris in Kanchipuram, 2012.

Source: Courtesy the photographer, Rags Raghavan.

of the fly-shuttle device in existing pit looms not only reduced the time required to weave a certain length of cloth, it also allowed broader cloths to be woven.

The fly-shuttle loom was aggressively popularised through 'peripatetic weaving parties' across the state.[41] And despite complaints of frequent snapping of threads on such looms, the fear of oversupply, competition from mills and power looms, and the special requirements of garments with borders which could not be woven on these looms, Chatterton and others worked hard at transforming the 'native' weaver's technology.[42]

Fig. 2.2: Fly-shuttle weaving of silk saris in Arani, 2013.
Source: Author.

Chatterton's indoctrination of the merits of the fly-shuttle loom was simultaneously propaganda against the traditional throw-shuttle pit loom which, in his view, was not productive enough to benefit the weaver. He proposed to rid the country loom of its technical inefficiency; not only would the fly-shuttle be more cost-effective (the setting up of the shuttle box and the slay frame could be simply attached to the existing loom), it would also enable handloom weavers to 'survive' the onslaught of competition from power looms and mills. The main argument in favour of the fly-shuttle loom being that it could turn out nearly twice as much work as the throw-shuttle loom, increasing the overall efficiency, and hence wages of the weaver in terms of the amount of yardage produced per unit time.

The fly-shuttle came to be extensively used in weaving running fabric as material for men's garments, especially in checks, towels, and home furnishing largely for export.[43] It was not ubiquitously adopted, however, as it proved to be inappropriate for weaving bordered cloth. This was recognised by Chatterton himself: 'The only cloths for which fly-shuttle looms have been found to be unsuitable so far are cloths with solid borders....'[44] 'In Conjeeveram, a large weaving centre ... the National Fund and Industrial Association have endeavoured to popularise the fly-shuttle loom, and I have assisted their efforts in so far that I have lent them six fly-shuttle handlooms, but the experiment has not been productive of any satisfactory result and the National Fund and Industrial Association have failed to popularise the fly-shuttle loom notwithstanding the fact that they fully recognise its merits.'[45]

Solid-border weaving on the handloom involves the hand-thrown shuttle technique using three shuttles in a single interlacing motion between the warp and the weft. In weaving with the fly-shuttle, the weft yarn forms the single unbroken thread passing from edge to edge at right angles to the warp. In three-shuttle weaving, however, the weft is discontinuous during a single shedding interval since each border has to be woven separately for solid colours to be obtained. The continued preference and revival in demand for such saris, particularly in silk, as we shall see, contributed greatly to its persistence despite reformist developments contrary to it.

CULTURAL REVIVAL: TASTE FOR THE TRADITIONAL

By the last quarter of the nineteenth century the design crisis in England, reflected in the Arts and Crafts Movement, brought to light the practical need for a reappraisal of 'oriental traditions' for the enhancement of Britain's own industrial design base.

India's 'applied' or 'decorative' art heritage came to be seen as a valuable standard of design for British manufacturers. The founding of the *Journal of Indian Art* in 1884 concretised the imperial state's recognition of the arts of its subject country. Artisanal products became synonymous with all that was 'traditional' in India for British art administrators such as Sir George Birdwood, Lockwood Kipling, Cecil Burns and Ernst B. Havell who actively engaged in 'the prevention of degradation' in the Indian arts in their search for authenticity.[46] Disparaging innovations and imitations as deviant, hybrid or spurious, they attributed the decline in the quality of craft products to the general tendency among native producers to digress from 'traditional' principles and standards of practice set by their forefathers.[47] Official interventions along these lines resulted in the establishment of museums, schools of art and the sponsoring of national exhibitions by the colonial government for the preservation and revival of interest in India's craft heritage.[48]

Around the same time, the philosophical idealism of Theosophists like Annie Besant and traditionalists like Coomaraswamy outside official circles had a profound influence on the rejuvenation of India's traditional culture embodied in the knowledge and practice of the Indian craftsman.[49] Coomaraswamy's nationalist valorisation of Indian art[50] was articulated through an awakening to the deterioration of public taste and sensibilities:

> It is as evil a thing for us to supply the American market with bales of cheap and vulgar phulkaris embroidered in offensive colours and mean designs and sloppy needlework as it is for Manchester to send us bicycle-patterned saris. The only true remedies that can be effectual are the re-generation of Indian taste, and the re-establishment of some standard of quality... Indian art can only revive and flourish if it is beloved by Indians themselves.[51]

His views posited India's craft tradition as archetypal of this enrichment that needed to be 'revived' not only for its own sake but also to cease the 'boycott of the Indian craftsman' whose way of life had to be safeguarded from the attack of modern industrialism.[52]

The official art policy in India, however, was that of public instruction in the applied arts that was employment-oriented and, when for export, in tune with European tastes. Modelled after schools of design in England, schools of art in India were set up to provide students with practical training in principles of design and technique with a distinct European bias. Havell challenged the prevailing system's bias in favour of European art history and the policy of importing art instructors from Britain and methods of training emphasising visual literacy and drawing techniques and sought to introduce the study of Indian art and craftsmanship as part of the curriculum.[53] Even though curricular reforms initiated by Havell replaced mediocre European art by pre-Renaissance art, and of fine examples from the Ajanta frescoes and the Mughal miniature tradition, students found 'little scope for their talents except in semi-clerical jobs as drawing masters, draughtsmen, engravers, lithographers and illustrators with the government.'[54] And despite efforts to revive local craft industries[55] and arrest their deterioration by setting standards of design and excellence, these schools failed to attract members of weaving castes.[56] Not only were they oriented to English-speaking students, the inherent bias for the fine arts and for modern scientific and technical training in these schools, together with their location in cities, humbled the very traditional crafts they were meant to promote.

In fact, the impetus to handloom weaving came from outside state-sponsored art and industrial promotion. It adopted the discourse of tradition to set new standards of taste and parameters of design for the solid-bordered silk hand-woven sari.

RE-AESTHETICISING TRADITION: THE KALAKSHETRA SARI

Yanagisawa's study of the handloom industry and its market structure in the Madras Presidency in early twentieth century indicates that changing dress codes among various classes created 'a new demand' for superior varieties, especially those in silk and gold thread. In 1912 a Japanese newspaper reported that 'the upper classes used silk cloth in everyday life in India and that as a result of an increase in their wealth and a rise in their standard of living, the consumption of silk goods in India was increasing.'[57] The adoption of brahminical dress conventions by members of the wealthier non-brahmin castes also meant an increase in demand for finer varieties of clothing in silk and gold lace. The *Manual of Tanjore District* (1883) attests that:

> Formerly, the use of Kornadu cloths was almost entirely restricted to the Tanjore Brahmans but now that Brahmanical customs are adopted generally by other higher classes and the inland traffic has been so much facilitated by Railways, these clothes find a market to a greater or less extent all over the south between the latitudes of Madras and Cape Comorin.[58]

The middle and lower classes, Yanagisawa notes, 'generally preferred to use artificial silk saris as they were cheaper than silk saris and had the same brightness and gloss ... for ceremonial purposes.'[59]

N. G. Ranga's report in the early decades of the twentieth century confirms this new trend in the handloom industry of the Madras Presidency:

> The substitution of silk weaving by artificial silk weaving has been effected in many places, while in other places cotton weaving has been replaced by silk weaving. It is largely true to say that weaving in rough cotton yarn has been given up in almost all places, its place being taken up by fine yarn, silk and artificial silk weaving.[60]

This trend disavowed nationalist appeals for producing and wearing khadi and found its legitimation in the discourse of cultural nationalism influenced by theosophy led by Annie Besant in Madras and the 'Tagore circle' at Calcutta.[61]

The revalorisation of handloom weaving and in particular the three-shuttle korvai technique was achieved at Kalakshetra in Madras through the efforts of Rukminidevi Arundale, whose own emergence as the adequately groomed champion of India's cultural renaissance was widely recognised not only in elite Madras society but also in wider national and international circles.[62] Modelled after the centre for arts set up by Rabindranath Tagore at Shantiniketan, *kala* meaning 'art' and *kshetra* meaning 'holy place' or 'field,' Kalakshetra was established in 1936 as an international academy of arts under the aegis of the Theosophical Society in Madras and aimed at inculcating high standards based on tradition in the arts. The resurrection of the *sadir attam*, the solo dance practised by *devadasis*[63], as the classical *bharatanatyam* dance of India and its move away from temples and elite homes to the modern public stage, was accompanied by the refinement of the dance sari.

At the time when Rukminidevi first danced on stage in the mid-1930s, brahmin women like herself were forbidden from appearing in any public performance in the arts. There was also the social stigma attached to the traditional practitioners of the dance because of a virulent anti-nautch campaign in the late nineteenth century.[64] The dress of the devadasi was considered equally unacceptable as it was, not only different from both brahmin and non-brahmin attire in Madras but also deemed vulgar due to its association with the dance. Only dancing girls wore blouses that enhanced their voluptuousness. And whereas all other castes wore unstitched garments, the devadasi wore ankle-length trousers beneath a distinctive drape: 'Dancing girls wear the cloth [sari] ... without passing it between the legs. These women also often wear drawers under their cloth reaching to the ankle and sometimes petticoats.'[65]

The rebirth of the dance of the devadasi on stage at Kalakshetra in the 1930s necessitated a new dance costume whose design and wearing style would appeal to the aesthetic and social sensibilities—both of the dancers and the upper-caste audience attending the performance.[66] The re-aesthetisation of the dance costume at Kalakshetra was part of the legitimating process of the dance of the devadasi and its sanskritised re-designation as 'classical.'[67] It was achieved through a purging of unrefined elements to suit the social

Fig. 2.3: Dancing girls in procession, Tanjore, water colour, c. 1820.
Source: Nevile 1996: 103.

respectability and aesthetic sensibilities of its new incumbent on stage. The re-signification of the dance sari at Kalakshetra in its new korvai avatar was achieved by grounding its design elements—texture, motifs, colours and border widths—in the familiar upper-caste idiom of the traditional, recovered through old samples collected from upper-caste households, temples, palaces and museums.

Rukminidevi commissioned dance saris to be woven in thick heavy silk with ornate gold thread embellishments as a strong departure from the ordinary cotton saris with simple borders that allowed their rather ornate and loud blouses and striped trousers to show through.[68] Within a year six pit looms were installed at the Weaving Unit in Kalakshetra and skilled silk sari weavers and their families were asked to re-locate from Kanchipuram.[69] Rukminidevi challenged the standard technique of *kuligai* [number of threads per unit space] calculations of the weavers and prescribed her own layouts and introduced new motifs in saris woven at Kalakshetra.

Shakuntala Ramani, who helped Rukminidevi set up the Weaving Centre at Kalakshetra, recalls the design interventions made by her:

The first sari which was put on the loom had an elaborate *zari thalaippu*.[70] The traditional motifs of deer, horse, trees, etc. which usually went into the weaving of this type of heavy gold brocade, was toned down and reduced to two, six inch panels of deer and flower motifs, separated by a wide coloured band of eight inches. In this space, a new motif of a row of parrots was introduced. The artist who drew ... the parrot was not familiar with weaving requirements. So sample pieces had to be produced, until the exact proportions of the motifs could be fixed.... The parrot was a favourite design....[71]

Fig. 2.4a and b: The weaving hall at Kalakshetra showing the frame looms upon which both silk and cotton Kalakshetra saris are woven. Generations of weavers from Chennai, Kanchipuram, Kumbakonam, Salem have come and settled here with their families.

Source: Author.

Silk was brought from Bangalore and twisted in the three-ply twist, yielding a texture characteristic of the saris already used as elite wear. The dyeing of the yarn, done at the Weaving Centre, was in deep contrasting colours made from vegetable dyes; the German chemical dyes were avoided in the nationalist spirit. Saris worn by Rukminidevi's own mother and those from other elite brahmin households were brought in for their motifs—*rudraksha*, the woody seed of the *Elaeocarpus ganitrus* tree used as a prayer bead and considered the sacred seed of Shiva; *mayilkannu* or peacock's eye; *pavun* or coin motif; *vanki*, a v-shaped pattern also named after an armband; *mangai* or mango; *tharzhampu*, the flower of the screw pine or *Pandanus* plant; *pillaiyar muggu*, the pagoda motif referring to Pillaiyar or Ganesha, the elephant-headed Hindu deity, in coloured silk and gold thread. These motifs—particularly the rudraksha and the mayilkannu (after which Mylapore, the brahmin-dominated area in Madras city is named)—were also found in men's cloths (*veshtis*) worn by upper castes at ritual occasions.[72]

The borders of saris woven at Kalakshetra were also altered to resonate with those of saris and veshtis worn by the upper castes in Madras. They consisted of two parallel lines of motifs six to seven inches apart (as in the brahmin saris) or in contrasting colours woven in the three-shuttle korvai technique commonly used for upper-caste men's wear and in saris worn by the high non-brahmin Nattukottai Chettiars. Members of the royal household at Chettinadu Palace in Madras contributed many a design for saris at Kalakshetra. Often their widths were broad and divided the entire sari into three equal parts along its length in the famous *munbaham* style associated with the dress of Chettiar ladies or *aachis*. The middle portion of the sari was treated in checks and stripes, in the manner of the elite wear already current. There was the *kottadi* or check with a matting effect in gold thread, *muthu-seer* or lines composed of dashes, *oosi-vanam*, the pin-stripe, quite common in the brahmin wedding sari, which was a shade of deep vermillion red with gold or *zari* work.

The *paalum-parzhamum* or 'milk and fruits,' a variegated check composed by the combination of lines in different sizes and also called the *visiri* or fan check, was common to the silk-mixed cotton saris of Kornadu in present day Thanjavur district of Tamil Nadu, favoured particularly by the Madhava brahmins in Mysore (now in Karnataka state). Another check popularly woven at Kalakshetra was the large sandal and black alternating squares described earlier on by Thurston in his industrial tour in 1887 as the 'High Court Papli' on account of its resemblance to the black and white tiles of the Madras High Court. These were greatly favoured by the Chettiars and old saris of similar description can be found even today in their homes. The end-piece of the saris to be worn for the dance performance were modelled after the elaborate zari brocades of Benaras and the courts of Mysore and Tanjore. Among these were the saris called *simhaasana* or 'royal throne' saris which featured the emblem of the Mysore maharaja—the double-headed eagle. Other figurative end-piece patterns included the horse, the lion, the peacock and the sacred *shombu*, a spherical water vessel.

Even the sari draping style of the devadasi was elevated to suit the new dancer whose upper-caste background necessitated adherence to norms of decency and modesty. The re-aestheticised dance muse was fashioned along the lines of an 'ancient temple dancer' whose virtue was equal to that of 'a pure and holy, sexually chaste woman ....'[73] Being brahmin herself, Rukminidevi was familiar with the *madisar-kattu* or 'pure drape' of the brahmins and used it as a model to re-imagine the devadasi's sari drape, now labelled as the *devadyaa-kattu*. While the devadasis wore pant-like garments, upper-caste Hindu women were forbidden from wearing garments that accentuated their legs. Women of lower castes, especially from farming communities, wore their saris higher up close to the knees; high-caste women on the other hand wore theirs close to the ankles. The crucial feature of the devadasi wearing style that needed to change was the sari's end-piece. It was considered to be highly suggestive as it was rarely secured or tucked in and generally left loose and flowing. Even the pleats of the devadasi's sari fell conspicuously in front and sometimes were sumptuously tucked in at the navel, forming a mango-shaped bulge referred to as the *maambazha-kattu* or 'mango-drape.'[74] This was in sharp contrast to the pleating style adopted by women from other castes which concealed the pleats, usually at the back or on the sides, by an additional wrap of the sari. It was believed that 'to have no folds at the back protecting the modesty of a woman was the mark and practice of public women ....'[75]

Rukminidevi's dance costumes on stage evolved over a period of time and included both sewn and draped sari-costumes, always made from the bright contrast-bordered silk saris woven at Kalakshetra. Her experiments in sari design were arbitrated by the notion of 'timeless appeal' and ultimately established indices of the traditional in the korvai silk sari.

With the emergence of classical bharatanatyam and its popularisation among the national elite, the dress of its highly acclaimed individual proponents soon began to be recognised as the dress of the cultured and educated elite Indian woman. The korvai sari was thus released from its specific regional identity, marked by specialised patronage, and began to appeal to other communities.

Kalakshetra's adherence to the 'traditional,' as redefined by Rukminidevi, helped shape a new national identity for the korvai sari, now increasingly referred to as a 'south silk,' an 'Adyar sari' or 'Kalakshetra sari' and began appealing to wider markets.[76] Upper-class women could now place orders for such saris at Kalakshetra, whose weavers could reproduce 'traditional' designs, colours and textures. The saris were woven strictly in accordance with Rukminidevi's instructions and could not be deviated from even if the client so wished. Rukminidevi was extremely particular not only about what she herself wore, but also of what was being woven at Kalakshetra. Members of the Kalakshetra family remember her expressing such strong displeasure upon finding a discordant colour or a motif being woven that she would have the sari immediately removed from the loom. The Weaving Centre was instructed to keep swatches of old saris for clients to choose from. Rukminidevi's private collection, still preserved at Kalakshetra, is testimony to her taste in bright colours, broad borders, checks and stripes and traditional motifs from the upper-caste dress repertoire.

Fig. 2.5: Bharatanatyam dancer Leela Samson with Rukminidevi Arundale on convocation day, 1 December 1970, at the Kalakshetra auditorium. She is wearing a copy of Rukminidevi's sari, the tender leaf-green body of which is contrasted with a dark brinjal-coloured border.

Source: Courtesy, Leela Samson.

The revivalist perspective in post-independence India, guided by Coomaraswamy loyalists, denounces mutations of tradition. This ideology continues to guide the documentation and display of saris in museums and exhibitions that cater to this elite sensitisation to the 'traditional.' Whereas the Crafts Museum exhorted weavers who came to demonstrate their skills at the museum's premises to abide with tradition,[77] state-sponsored Weaver's Service Centres encouraged local weavers to innovate through design development within the parameters dictated by tradition. In both cases the revivalist perspective guided weavers to adhere to the new definition of 'traditional' through a regionalisation of craft designs legitimised by 'policy communities' comprising nationalist social elites and designers[78] via exhibitions like 'Master Weavers,' 'Visvakarma' and special exhibitions and sales exclusively featuring 'Kalakshetra' designs. The 'Saris of India' series of books sponsored by the Development Commissioner for Handlooms during the last decade of the twentieth century was part of this national revival and re-definition of regional Indian sari styles.

The national cultural preservationist agenda was now poised for export outside the country through 'Festivals of India' abroad. India was represented as a 'crafts nation,' her range of handlooms as diverse and unique as its people.[79] Exhibitions abroad featured the versatile Indian sari in all its regional variations. Reinstating the classical korvai sari through the diorama of international fashion shows, as the style preference of Miss India abroad, or Miss World in India, are efforts aimed at achieving national uniqueness for a regional textile tradition. The transnational circulation of global media, fashion and capital since the closing decade of the twentieth century continues to adhere to this sensibility of tradition.[80] It contrasts the modernity of mill-made saris popular among the lower and middle classes[81] only to reinforce the significance of the hand-made among elite patrons and designers who consciously state the saris' identity and departure from roots within a regional handloom tradition.[82]

The colonial privileging of a particular handloom technique fuelled the emergence of a market for silk saris following the standards of design set by Kalakshetra in the period after independence. Between 1950 and 1997, power looms made only 'hesitant inroads' into established community-based clusters of silk handloom weaving in south India. Roy notes for instance that:

> In the Sourashtra-dominated town of Madurai town, the shift from traditional handloom cloth to power loom is seen as too violent a break with custom, not only in a psychological way, but also in skills, employment practices, marketing, contacts and networks, and with the community's past which carries a brand image in a handloom cloth.[83]

Instead, silk sari production expanded outside institutional settings and drew upon caste and kin networks of handloom organisation.

ENDNOTES

1. See Prasad (2001) for an expansive reading of Gandhi's experiments in cloth. The work demonstrates how khadi embodied experiments in grass roots mobilisation through the juxtaposition of science and artisanal practice by Gandhian workers.
2. Gandhi 1925: 414.
3. Extracts from this speech were also published as 'The Fallacy of Handloom Weaving' in *Young India*, 13 October 1927 (Gandhi 1969: 58–9).
4. Gandhi 1921: 68.
5. Rajaji was influenced by Gandhi's views and attempted to introduce Gandhi's scheme of Basic (craft-based) Education during his tenure as the Chief Minister of the Madras Presidency of British India (1937–39). It was rejected by his political opponents and derisively interpreted as the *kula kalvi thittam* or 'hereditary/caste-based education policy.'
6. Quoted in Rangarajan et al 2014: 234–5; 329.
7. The origin and growth of sericulture in south India has been attributed to official experimentation and promotion both by the East India Company in the Madras Presidency and by Tipu Sultan in the State of Mysore from the nineteenth century. The industry became

somewhat stable between the period 1910 to 1940 and it was only during World War II with the demand for parachutes that the acreage under mulberry cultivation expanded considerably, making south Karnataka and the contiguous districts of Tamil Nadu and Andhra Pradesh the leading silk producers in the country (Charsley 1982: 78; Sinha 1990: 7).

8. Handler and Linnekin 1984; Bayly 1988; Ludden 1993; Washbrook 1997.

9. Dirks 2001 and McGowan 2009.

10. Bayly 2001: 215.

11. Caste became a bureaucratic category for the award or denial of favours in public employment and political representation (Carroll 1978).

12. In the early years of the twentieth century a representative of the Vishwarkarma community is known to have petitioned before the Industrial Commission, resisting the bias in selection of students for training abroad. He argued that scholarships should favour students 'who possess the initial aptitude for manual labour' i.e. those belonging to hereditary manual professions rather than those with literary proficiency (Visvanathan 1985: 57).

13. 'The Vizagpatnam collector reported that sudras made excellent engineers .... The Ganjam collector recorded that "brahmins are good in an office, but not so useful in the hard out of door life that an engineer should lead" ...' (Radhakrishnan 1993: 1588).

14. Weber 1948: 401.

15. Karuna Miryam's work significantly sheds light on the internal hierarchy among weaving groups in south India. In the Madras Presidency for instance, 'All castes considered to be weavers were grouped under the heading Kaikolar on the logic that the Kaikala (or Kaikolar) was the predominant weaving caste in the Presidency. Pariahs or Malas find no place in this list' (Miryam 2014: 18). The distinction extended to patterns of residence so that '... for the region around Colar, while weavers from the Devanga and Shayniga castes ("specialist" weaving castes) lived in the town, the Whalliaru were found in surrounding villages. In Silagutta, the "specialist" Padma Shalay weavers lived in the town while Whalliaru weavers occupied the hinterland' (ibid.: 8).

16. In this system of pre-capitalist production in Europe, the merchant clothier advanced ('put-out') raw materials to the weaver in his domestic workshop, paid him piece-work wages and exclusively owned the products of his labour (Thompson 1963; Bythell 1969; Goody 1982).

17. The spatialisation of artisanal products to specific places of production within a cartography of craft production in the idiom of the traditional is taken up in some detail in chapter 6.

18. Baker 1981: 587.

19. Chatterton gave his recommendations in E. Buck's *Report on Practical and Technical Education* (1901). Class V referred to 'Manual work schools on the "disciplinary" system which prepare boys by manual exercises for manual occupations' and Class VII were the 'Special trade schools not giving literary instruction for teaching improvements in an industry or for teaching a new industry under school officials. These were the Sericulture school in Bengal; the Aluminium school in Madras; Art Schools in Bengal, Madras, Bombay and Punjab' (quoted in Swaminathan 1992: 1612; 1621).

20. Chatterton 1912: 335–6.

21. Report 1908: 21–3.

22. Chatterton 1912: 218.

23. Venkataraman 1940: 71–2.

24. In 1910, opposition from the private sector to state intervention in its own sphere prompted the Industrial Commission to redefine the role of the state from one engaging in commercial ventures to that of a technological innovator and pedagogic facilitator (Visvanathan 1985). Alfred Chatterton was transferred to the post of Superintendent of Industrial Education under the Director of Public Instruction.

25. Havell [1912] 1986: 179.

26. Ibid.: 191.

27. Ibid.: 184–5.

28. Ibid.: 180.

29. Visvanathan 1985: 58.

30. This body was the precursor to Co-optex, the present apex body functioning above all cooperative societies in the state. The latter's objective is to provide weavers a steady supply of yarn and assured sales for their cloths through its vast state-wide network of Primary Societies.

31. The khadi campaign's stress on hand-woven and handspun cloth, i.e. hand-woven cloth that did not employ mill yarn (which handloom weavers were using) proved disheartening for weavers in Madras, and the state government in 1937–39 pursued a 'dual policy of encouraging both industry and handicrafts' (Irschick 1986: 243–4).

32. Havell 1902, 1908, 1912; Report 1908; Chatterton 1912; Amalsad 1925; Narayana Rao 1925; Ranga 1930; Venkataraman 1940; Narayanaswami Naidu 1948; Narayanaswami Pillai 1955.

33. This was the time when the Indian government had begun to levy a small cess on Indian mill-made cloth to subsidise the cloth woven on handlooms. 'Money from the Government of India to the Madras government was only Rs. 26,500 in 1934–35 for the handloom subsidy, but in the following year it was Rs. 59,500' (Irschick 1986: 244).

34. Arterburn's study (1982) on the administrative structure of weavers' cooperative societies in Tamil Nadu shows how state appointed government officials rather than members of weavers communities form the board of managing directors: 'Non-weavers have been appointed as presidents in all new societies because the government believes the weavers lack the business and managerial experience necessary for managing a new cooperative' (Arterburn 1982: 127).

35. Mitter 1977; Visvanathan 1985; Metcalf 1989; Sundar 1995.

36. Report 1908: 45–6.

37. Havell's (1912) account of the feasibility of apparatuses invented by Messrs. Hattersley in the Indian context demonstrates this line of intervention. Peg warping, the slasher-sizer and the warping mill were being used in many weaving hamlets in Tamil Nadu in the 1980s and 90s.

38. Roy 2002: 527–8.

39. Report 1908: 4.

40. In modern looms the mechanism that transmits the weft across the warp is extremely sophisticated. There are shuttle-stop machines that can control the shuttle mid-way between the warp and even shuttle-less weaving machines in which the weft flies across the warp propelled by air and water jets (Talavasek and Svaty 1981).

41. These touring groups aimed at bringing the advantages of the fly-shuttle to weavers at their doorstep. The service was started in 1911 and withdrawn by 1932 (Baker 1984: 406).

42. From 20,000 looms in 1912, by the mid-30s the number of looms equipped with the fly-shuttle in Madras rose to a staggering seventy per cent of the province's total of some 300,000 looms (Baker 1984: 395).

43. cf. Swallow 1982.

44. Report 1908: 4.

45. Chatterton 1912: 230.

46. Quoted in McGowan 2005: 273.

47. Ibid.

48. The Asiatic Society Museum in Calcutta was the first of its kind to be supported by the state in 1839. About a dozen museums had been set up by the middle of the nineteenth century in major cities like Madras, Bombay, Karachi (Sundar 1995: 103). The imperial government later extended an educational function to these museums, which were seen to serve as repositories of superior examples of Indian craftsmanship as reference material for future talents and tastes (ibid.: 131).

49. Stella Kramrisch, an American art historian deeply influenced by Hindu metaphysics and the theosophy of Rudolf Steiner, was also responsible for shaping traditionalist views of the Indian craftsman. She attributed the knowledge of the universal 'Principle' of creative consciousness to the craftsman and which, she held, was imparted through 'tradition' (Kramrisch 1959).

50. Coomaraswamy 1909a; 1909b; 1911.

51. Coomaraswamy [1909a] 1981: 77.

52. Coomaraswamy 1911: 24.

53. Tarapor 1980; Metcalf 1989; Sundar 1995; Tarar 2011.

54. Sundar 1995: 149.

55. The School of Arts in Madras added to its curriculum decorative metal work, wood carving, cabinet making, furniture and architectural woodwork, pottery, glass manufacture and carpet-weaving (Swaminathan 1992: 1617).

56. A weaving school opened in 1915 as part of the colonial government's efforts to organise silk weaving in Benaras also did not attract members of the weaving castes (Kumar 1988: 23).

57. Yanagisawa 1993: 22. Some members of the elite, however, opted to wear *ahimsa* or 'non-violent' silks following Gandhian ideals (ibid.: 109).

58. Cited in Yanagisawa 1993: 22.

59. Ibid.: 24.

60. Ranga, 1930: i.

61. According to Mark Frost, the 'Tagore Circle' was the cosmopolitan arena for intellectual discussions around pan-Asianism led by Tagore, Okakura, Coomaraswamy and Sister Nivedita: 'In a sense, the founding constitution of the Visva□Bharati University represents the Tagore circle's closing manifesto on Asian unity' (Frost 2011: 33).

62. Srinivasan 1985.

63. Literally 'women in service of the lord,' belonging to the Tamil *isai vellala* community engaged in the hereditary practice of music and dance.

64. The anti-nautch agitation of the late-nineteenth and early-twentieth century had called for a ban of the devadasi dance from temples and people's homes on moral grounds (Srinivasan 1985).

65. Madras Presidency, Tanjore district Gazetteer, 1906: 64.

66. Srinivasan (1985) has shown how the devadasi herself was systematically divorced from the practice of her dance. The new dancers were recruited from among elite, urban, Western-educated women, as they are indeed even today—the very section of society which had been attracted to theosophy in the first place.

67. Coorlawala refers to this process as 'sanskritisation' following M. N. Srinivas whereby 'dance forms designated as "ritual", "folk", or simply insignificant, attain social and politico-artistic status' (Coorlawala 2004: 53–4).

68. These were stitched in fabrics woven by the admixture of silk and cotton yarn in stripes (referred to as *kuthini*), also used to make pillows and cushions, and were commonly worn by Muslims and other non-brahmin sections of the society (Thurston 1899; Madras Presidency, Tanjore district Gazetteer, 1906: 118).

69. This paralleled the shifting of the renowned dance guru of the devadasis, Meenakshi Sundaram Pillai from his village in Pandanallur in Tanjore district to Kalakshetra in Madras (Srinivasan 1985).

70. This refers to the end-piece of a sari woven with gold-plated yarn. In Tamil Nadu the words *thalaippu* or *mundaani* are commonly used to refer to the *pallav*, which is a north-Indian term for the elaborate end-piece of a sari and understood throughout India.

71. Ramani 2002: 75.

72. See, for instance, the famed Salem *mayilkannu veshti* in red and green borders used even today as the most formal men's garment.

73. Srinivasan 1985: 1875.

74. Ghurye 1951: 211.

75. Ibid.

76. See chapter 6 for a further discussion on shifts in patterns of consumption of the silk korvai sari and its changing rhetoric of value.

77. cf. Greenough 1996.

78. DeNicola 2004.

79. Greenough 1996: 242.

80. Runkle 2004.

81. Banerjee and Miller 2004.

82. See for instance Kapur-Chishti et al 2000; Katiyar 2009.

83. Roy 1998: 899.

THREE

SUSTAINING PRODUCTION
Leadership and Cooperative Conflicts

Handloom weaving involves not only the technology of weaving, the loom equipment and its functionalities, the procurement of dyed yarn and its preparation for the loom, but also the pattern of social arrangements that foster their use and permit continuation of the productive processes. Focusing on the social geography[1] of silk handloom weaving in Tamil Nadu led me to supra-local kin-based networks of production and distribution linking wholesale silk sari producers in Kanchipuram and Kumbakonam to major silk retailers in Chennai. These weaving towns are not only the foci for distribution of dyed silk yarn along with the technical specifications to weavers from neighbouring villages but also collection points of saris woven in hundreds of weaving households in their vicinity. Such a model of distributed production depends on caste-based work identities as the primary frame of reference for the mobilisation and sustenance of capital and labour.

In the 70s when Arterburn conducted field work among the silk weaving cooperatives in Kanchipuram, a shared caste background was essential for ensuring that the benefits of capital were not entirely antithetical to the interest of weavers.[2] She notes the resilience of small producer-merchants despite communist appeals of '*all* weavers as exploited labourers' as part of the cooperative movement in Kanchipuram.[3] Weaving as a common hereditary privilege and livelihood option predisposed organisers of production in understanding the needs of weavers, to serve as administrators in the silk cooperatives and in turn be accepted by weaver members in this capacity. Moreover, these merchant wholesalers were not far removed from weaving. They were former weavers who continued to keep looms in their homes, reside in weaving neighbourhoods and who were recognised as leaders in the weaving profession on account of their struggle to achieve financial success.

By the 1990s small producers or wholesale weaver-merchants of silk saris in Kanchipuram were in their heyday and Padma Saliyars among them were recognised for their technical skills in silk weaving.[4] There were many weavers who had reaped the silk boom and had begun employing weavers and apprentices from non-weaving backgrounds to ply the looms in their homes so that they could be freed to organise credit for the yarn and secure orders from buyers in Chennai. My interest in the articulation of caste among the Padma Saliyars led me to focus on codes of conduct that underlie unequal relations of capital and labour in handloom weaving. I shall focus on their practise of using strategic marriage partnerships in building and expanding a supra-local network of production to illuminate communal arrangements both inside and outside the household. The genealogies I collected pointed to a dynamic rather than rigid network of caste, kin and neighbourhood ties. They support productive processes that link big silk sari retailers in Chennai with wholesale producers in Kanchipuram and Kumbakonam who in turn offer contracts to weaving households in a number of villages in their vicinity.

The stability and survival of this distributed production matrix involve 'cooperative conflicts'[5] and refer to the milieu of cooperation within which conflicting interests are mediated. I use Amartya Sen's phrase to refer to the bargaining power and respective positions of the different actors involved in productive arrangements both inside and outside the weaving household. Here getting a fair deal means choosing a mutually beneficial configuration till a more feasible arrangement for all concerned is found. It is in the best interests of the parties seeking productive outcomes to endure the uneven productive relationships in periods of expansion as well as in times of distress and attrition. In households with more than one adult weaver the looms are often dedicated to different producers and at least one loom is dedicated to a local cooperative society. This is to offset the risks involved with a single source of income and in leveraging subsistence support during lean periods.

The resilience of the differentially valued labouring and non-labouring activities in handloom production depends on acts of cooperation that sustain the arrangement even during overt situations of conflict. In a weaving household, for instance, gender-based cooperative conflicts refer not so much to unequal role-based entitlements but to the general well-being and sustenance of the household. Viewed thus, pre-loom activities of winding and spinning the yarn in preparation for the loom are not subsidiary to weaving and, like other undertakings of the household such as food preparation and childcare, are essential for its daily maintenance.

Women have equal access to train on the loom and contribute to the household earning through it even though they do not automatically inherit the instrument of production upon marriage. They are therefore equally adept at weaving and are often full-time weavers depending upon the social arrangements within the working household.[6]

For the Padma Saliyars it is not unusual for the alleged feminine domains such as the hearth, ritual and marriage to surpass the domain of the private and enter the public realm with significant economic and political dimensions. Marriage among the Padma Saliyars is not merely a means of social reproduction but the expansion of one's arena of control and influence in the weaving profession. A daughter-in-law from a weaving background is considered to be an asset because she will be proficient in managing the work of the household. It is even more strategic to establish affinal ties with a family of weaving repute even if it means searching for a suitable alliance among distantly located caste members.[7] Padma Saliyars engaged in handloom production regularly make such considered matches through advertisements in the monthly magazine run by the caste association for a small annual subscription. Indeed, marrying outside of one's caste group is not a personal matter but a social violation requiring the consent of caste elders. The professional status of a daughter-in-law's natal family and her own prowess in weaving matters often mark her relative position and bargaining power in her husband's family.

Marriage creates a fiduciary relationship between weaving families. Weavers from the network of villages under a producer can be asked to weave for an affine, if so desired, making the output of additional looms (rather than the actual looms themselves) transferable. The strategic union of two weaving families not only has material rewards in terms of an expanded production base but also symbolic gains in the form of future credit and social honour in a widening circle of community ties. Equally, the fissioning of households occurs along the male line and involves partitioning of the family's loom base at the time of marriage and a consequent loss of resources until another opportune alliance is made. The dynamic base of cooperative conflicts ensures that expansion *and* contraction of the social technology of production surpasses the rigid structural antagonisms of gender, class and caste associated with other forms of productive organisation. Supporting an expansive production network of silk handloom saris is therefore seen by the Padma Saliyars as the mark of a leader, whose tangible achievements of material fulfilment and social eminence through the weaving profession vindicate a shared hereditary privilege.

BUILDING COMMUNITY: LEADERSHIP AND HONOUR

Leadership appears as the organising principle mediating the tension between individual and collective interests and aspirations at every level of handloom production and distribution—the micro level of weaving households in villages, the middle level of wholesale producers in towns and the macro level of city-based big retailers. The collective recognition of big and small Padma Saliyar silk sari producers in the caste association bears testimony to their ascendance as respected leaders (*talevars*) of the community. Office bearers in the history of national, state, district and village-level Padma Saliyar associations are remembered for their contribution in mobilising social, educational and economic constituencies for the community and cited as leaders in bringing visibility to the caste group as a whole.

A senior member of the Tamil Nadu Sangam in Chennai recalls that the first *Padmasali Bahu-uttama Sangama Pathashala* or 'caste association school' was started under the guidance of Nukala Venkata Subbiah in 1911, a district-level education official in Pullampettai in Cuddapah district in the British Presidency of Madras. He organised the first All India Padmasali Association[8] with the support of caste leaders, including Kariampudi Venkata Krishnakavi, and was to hold its first conference (*mahasabha*) at Pullampettai in 1921. In Tamil Nadu the different district-level associations are linked with prominent Padma Saliyar individuals whose leadership role in rallying caste fellows is recorded in various publications brought out by the caste association. The discussions at the weekly meetings at the Chennai office of the Tamil Nadu Padma Saliyar Sangam revealed that local caste associations survived as long as their respective leaders were able to muster financial support from wealthy members of the caste which was in turn dependent upon the latitude and weight of their kin and affinal network. The endurance of local caste associations, indeed their vitality, is mirrored in the ebb and flow of the fortunes of its leaders.

Drawing from the history of the association charted by its members, Table 3.1 below maps the different district-level Padma Saliyar associations in Tamil Nadu and the years during which they were bolstered by different handloom leaders of the community.[9]

Table 3.1: District-level Padma Saliyar caste associations in Tamil Nadu, with years of commencement and leaders

District-level caste association	*Year of commencement*	*Padma Saliyar leaders*
Salem	1925, 1945, 1946 and 1970	Venkata Subbiahgaru, R. V. Narasimhalu Chettiar, Arcot Kuppusami Chettiar, S. K. Yerana Chettiar, and reconvened once again by R. V. Narasimhalu Chettiar.
Kanchipuram	1927 and 1974	Pattalai Chinnasami Chettiar, Varadappa Chettiar, A. K. Chengalvaraya Chettiar, P. Chinnasami Chettiar. Reconvened by N. Nalli Chettiar, P. V. Jayaraman Chettiar, Nalli C. Duraiswamy Chettiar.
Madurai (Siddapattni, Vadaghapatti)	1948	K. K. Govindaramanujan
Tiruchirapalli (Thennarkaadu)	1973	D. Govindasami, S. R. Nagarasu Chettiar
Thanjavur	1976	Sembianmalai Rajagopala Chettiar, Injikollai Kannabiran, Kumbakonam S. R. G. Ranganathan Chettiar, Aduthurai S. R. Govindarajulu Chettiar.
Chennai	1974, 1976, 1979, 1982, 1987, 1994, 2002	R. Kodantharaman of Radha Silks, A. V. Puniyakoti Chettiar of Gemini Lungi Co., Manavallan/Mallavatha Venkatapa Chettiar of Bharatha Handloom House, Nalli Kuppuswami Chettiar, Kancha R. Purushottaman of Attur, Salem, K. G. Ramaswami Chettiar of KGR Silks in Kumbakonam.

Source: Author.

Padma Saliyar caste associations in the smallest ward or municipality indicate the presence of locally elected office-bearers and serve as platforms for their demonstrated ability to organise production and sustain a number of weaving households in the locality. The caste-based mobilisation among Padma Saliyar leaders is not the same as the culture of political constituency building around the figure of a charismatic individual in Tamil Nadu, studied by Pandian (1992) and Dickey (1993). Leadership among the Padma Saliyars also differs from that of the person-centred 'institutional big-man,' as defined by Mines and Gourishankar (1990), whose authority is enacted through a variety of institutions that he creates and controls and whose charismatic style is sanctioned by a specific cultural model of galactic polity.

Recognition by an expansive constituency of caste members is central to the establishment of a leader in Padma Saliyar handloom publics.[10] Revisionist textile historiography has clarified that the 'head' weaver in late colonial south India, who was likened to the European guild 'master' organising cloth production and employing many journeymen, was in fact an elected village-level leader of a weaving caste. He played the role of a social mediator with fiduciary responsibilities and did not have absolute control over production. Similarly, referring to the territorial organisation or the *naadu* system among the Kaikkoolars in Tamil Nadu, Mines points out that 'the officers of the naaDus (sic) settled disputes, and appear to have thought themselves to be their localities' rightful brokers, regulating interlocality trade. However, they administered only what passed through the system. They had no control over production.'[11] While both material and symbolic capital is gained through the development of a supra-local network of production, the voluntary acceptance of fiduciary duties towards the larger community via the caste association is the mark of a Padma Saliyar leader.[12]

The continuing relevance of caste is also evident in the practice of leadership which is not merely a matter of political brokerage or mobilisation of labour but a form of patron-like sociality that permeates and sustains everyday work and community life. It involves presiding at naming ceremonies, marriages, religious functions, temple donations and renovations, providing scholarships and distributing books and stationary to students, setting up facilities for daily feeding of the elderly and poor, arbitrating between disputants, petitioning the Government of Tamil Nadu on matters pertaining to the silk handloom industry, staging protests and fasts and so on. Leadership within a network of supra-local production and distribution guarantees benefits (and obligations) within a hierarchical arrangement, but the rigidity and severity of these relations are mitigated through the caste association that facilitates inter-local and supra-local relations within a communal framework comprising caste-based kin and affines.

The different tiers of the caste association and its leaders spatialise the community in Tamil Nadu whose periodic affirmation and renewal is evident in the bestowal of honours at public events and ceremonies.[13] My first such event was in August 1995 in Kumbakonam where I was witness to the sixtieth birthday celebrations of K. G. Ramaswami Chettiar (henceforth KGR), the then President of the Tamil Nadu Padma Saliyar Sangam. It was attended by more than five thousand Padma Saliyars from across the state, including some leaders from Andhra Pradesh and Karnataka. KGR had organised the largest state-level Padma Saliyar conference to coincide with his sixtieth birthday celebrations. The expenses for this meeting were entirely borne by him. The fact that prominent Padma Saliyars, notably silk businessmen from Chennai, were also present at the occasion was a collective recognition of KGR's role as a trustworthy leader of the supra-local community. He was acknowledged not only for his role in the productive chain of silk handloom saris but also on account of his acceptance of a fiduciary duty towards the wider group. KGR's particularly competent role in developing a viable network of weaving households across the district made him eligible for the honour of upholding a hereditary privilege and shaped his leadership status within the caste group.[14] Indeed, professional leadership in a spatially defined arena of work practice establishes an individual's reputation as *yokkiyamaana*, or one who is worthy of respect, and ultimately forms the basis for the conferral of *mariyaathai*, or honour, among Padma Saliyars in Tamil Nadu.

The historiography of handloom production in south India has shown that caste has been the locus for collective bargaining since the eighteenth century.[15] Weavers' protests included many everyday forms of collective resistance such as deserting entire villages overnight and migrating to different locales for employment, to prevent peasantisation or as a way to survive famines. Weavers who chose to take advances from merchants also demonstrated a degree of dynamism and strategic agency. They did so not so much on account of paucity of funds as to compel merchants 'to bear some of the risks associated with cloth production. These risks included uncertainties in the prices of yarn and cloth, shortages of yarn, droughts and localized shortfalls of grain. A merchant who made an advance to a weaver had to share the burden of losses resulting from economic fluctuations ....'[16] Such a dispersal of risk meant the mutual accretion and decline of the fortunes of weavers and merchants. It also ensured alternating ties of dependence and security so that 'when the weaver prospered, the merchant prospered' and equally of power and agency when 'the merchant reduces the money, the weaver reduces the thread.'

THREE LEVELS OF SUPRA-LOCAL PRODUCTION

Leadership among the Padma Saliyars in Tamil Nadu is evidenced along three spatially distinct levels of silk sari production and is continually made visible through public acts of patronage and allegiance to the group via the caste association. The micro, middle and macro levels correspond to relations pertaining to numerous weaving households in Padma Saliyar dominated streets in villages; in the towns of Kumbakonam and Kanchipuram where a few leaders have the capacity to raise funds to organise production in these villages, forming a cluster around a thirty-kilometre radius; and in the city of Chennai where still fewer, prominent Padma Saliyar silk business houses with access to national and international markets retail sari stocks sourced from these producers. Relations within each level are competitive but occur within a substratum of shared values, kin relationships and codes of conduct that defend a hereditary right to weave. Exchange between the levels takes place across designated relations of contract so that a weaver nearly always deals with producers in nearby towns and never directly with macro-level retailers in cities.

The legitimacy of this pyramid-like formation of levels of leadership in the organisation of silk sari production derives from the assumption that hereditary knowledge of, and practical experience in, the weaving profession is a marker of competence in specified arenas of action. In Kanchipuram for instance, highly skilled Padma Saliyar weavers are known for their ability to manipulate the loom apparatus to weave complex patterns in silk and gold. According to an official of a silk cooperative society, hereditary silk sari weavers cannot be persuaded into doing simpler designs as weaving a wedding sari for them is a 'status issue,' even a 'birth-right.' Similarly, the few Padma Saliyar-owned regional silk sari houses with outlets in major cities in the country as well as abroad are known for their business acumen and long-standing relations with customers as are middle-level Padma Saliyar leaders recognised for their prowess in raising capital and organising production.

The transition from being a weaver of silk saris to being responsible for their production and sale in expansive markets is a prospect open to more than a privileged few. Social mobility through the handloom profession is common on account of flexible productive arrangements mediated by caste. Accumulating capital, engaging contract weavers and keeping a pulse on market trends are skills and capabilities that can be acquired and honed by anyone with a demonstrated ability for taking on leadership roles in the community. There are aspirants to leadership positions at every spatial level of sari production in Tamil Nadu and each level is characterised by distinct spheres of control, action and influence. At the level of the weaving household and street, for instance, the primary aspiration is to retain one's autonomy and control over the weaving process and the products of the loom and to expand one's social credit in the neighbourhood through concrete acts of mediation and responsibility on behalf of other Padma Saliyar households.

I have chosen to demonstrate the elasticity of productive arrangements in silk handloom production among the Padma Saliyars through an examination of the biographies of three individuals belonging to each of the three spatially distinct levels. Whereas the caste association and its handloom public establishes and maintains the social parameters for cooperation, competition between individuals occurs in terms of the number of looms they control, the degree of autonomy enjoyed in their respective work spheres and the extent of their influence in wider society. The Tamil referential term *Chetti* or *Chettiar*—used as a suffix for silk leaders at all levels of production—defends rights to mobility within the group as well as within the wider caste hierarchy.

Micro Level: Weaving Households in Villages and Small Towns

J. Nathamuni Chetti (1941–2000), Swamimalai, Thanjavur District

Sometime during the 1930s, Nathamuni's father, Jagannatha Chetti, migrated from village T. Pallur (in Tiruchirapalli district) to Swamimalai (eight kilometres from Kumbakonam) in response to the growing demand for weavers of mixed silk and cotton Kornadu saris. He took up residence with his family on West Raja Street and installed two pit looms in the house. By the mid-1950s, the two looms in their household, as well as those in most other Padma Saliyar weaving households like theirs, began to weave exclusively for K. G. Ramaswami (KGR), a middle level silk sari producer from Kumbakonam. After their father's death in early 1960, Nathamuni and his younger brother, Ranganathan, continued to weave for KGR on these looms. When Ranganathan got married in the early 1970s, the loom assets had to be divided between the two brothers. Ranganathan moved to a house in East Vadampokki

Street and began taking orders independently of Nathamuni. A new loom was installed in the pit originally allocated to Ranganathan in the parental house for Nathamuni's wife to independently complete orders received by the household. In the late 1980s Nathamuni and his wife added a third loom in their home for wage-weavers to work under their supervision.

The looms in a weaver's household are classified as *sonda nesavu tari* or loom woven upon by oneself and *coolie nesavu tari* or loom woven upon by a daily wage-weaver or *coolies* who receive a piece-wage that varies according to the skill and quality of weaving required per sari woven. In the mid-90s nearly sixty of the ninety Padma Saliyar households in Swamimalai owned the looms in their homes on the basis of which they could take *oppandam* or contractual orders from middle-level producers. About twenty of these weavers were able to even purchase the raw material and independently organise production on their looms. Of the some 110 looms in Padma Saliyar households, at least one third of these looms were woven upon by hired labour and the remaining seventy-four were used by members of Padma Saliyar weaving households.

When I first met Nathamuni, each of the three looms in his home was committed to weave to three different Padma Saliyar producers from Kumbakonam. The oppandam or contract entails receiving raw materials or cash advance for weaving saris from middle-level producers, and does in no way alter Nathamuni's ownership of these looms. A loom is said to be under the 'contract' of a middle level producer till such time as the designated warp, or lengthwise threads laid upon the loom's horizontal axis, is being woven to its specifications.

Once the order is completed and the payments settled against advances received, Nathamuni is free to use the same loom for fresh orders and equally to dismantle the apparatus during lean times. Unlike loom-less weavers working on daily wages, Nathamuni must bear the liability of any weaving defects in the sari. It is in his interest to ensure that the quality of the raw material as well as the finished product is not compromised. At the same time, his mastery in weaving elaborate gold brocade designs and in carefully executing the korvai border weave is a skill not easily acquired and requires years of training and experience. As a reputed silk sari weaver, Nathamuni is highly sought after and is known to attempt any complex weave expected of him. He is valued not only for his expertise but also for his reliability in satisfactorily completing sari orders in the stipulated time period.

The work schedule in a weaver's household is not easily amenable to calculations on a daily, weekly or even monthly basis and often varies with the annual Tamil Hindu festival and ritual calendar. Some months are characterised by a heavy weaving load, while others are lean either because it is raining or because the wedding season is over. This means that the time spent on weaving and the final output in terms of saris woven must be adjusted over a period of time. The income and expenditure of the household is estimated according to the number of warps received per household, which in turn depends on the number of looms in the house. Nathamuni has the flexibility to rotate both funds and yarn by staggering and prioritising weaving cycles of one loom over another in order to manage the household finances. He is also in a position to decline orders if the cash advances are not as expected, or if it involves design specifications incompatible with his loom apparatus. In 1972 when KGR lost control of looms in Swamimalai to another to middle-level producer, N. Kannan, Nathamuni did not immediately shift allegiances. This was the time when Nathamuni was in the process of resolving the conflict with his younger brother over the ownership of looms. N. Kannan was not only impatient in the completion of sari orders but also refused to give Nathamuni an advance to finance his brother's marriage. In the meantime, Nathamuni was sought out by yet another Padma Saliyar producer from Kumbakonam, S. R. G. Ranganathan Chetti, who helped him tide over the crisis with a generous advance.

Nathamuni's household is a valued training ground for apprentices from non-weaving backgrounds in and around Swamimalai. The young girls who come to weave on the third loom are treated like members of the household and, in turn, they see themselves as having gained training and work experience from a reputed weaving household. Quite unlike the factory-like discipline of the weaving shed where more than twenty looms are housed under the same roof, their timings are not stringent as long as the requisite number of saris are woven in a given time period. Even the atmosphere is one of camaraderie rather than strict supervision. In fact, for Nathamuni and his wife, hiring outside help is a way of having a 'full house' and a convivial atmosphere to work in. It ensures that weaving continues without interruption in their home and lends their own work schedule some flexibility. Nathamuni and his wife are able to fulfil their social commitments and also maintain an average of completing one warp (six saris) in two months.

Weavers, according to Nathamuni, must not be judged on the basis of the distinction between 'good' and 'bad' weaving practice. For him, 'all Padma Saliyars are good [i.e., both skilled and trustworthy] weavers,' and one can either possess the skill of silk weaving or not. Nathamuni's defence of patrimony belies his own reputation of being highly skilled and trustworthy in his dealings and points to distinctions between recognised degrees of expertise and reliability. Middle-level producers acknowledge that 'when Nathamuni brings a sari to us we never check for defects.' His skill in the accurate execution of minute designs in the end-piece and expertise in weaving korvai borders with exacting precision and neatness is well regarded. Nathamuni himself insists on 'laying his cards out in the open' and is explicit about what he can and cannot do in terms of the skill required and the demands of his own time schedule before accepting orders. A weaver's *thozhil dharma* or work ethic in Nathamuni's terms is to maintain the trust of the client and integrity of the received warp by ensuring that the designated loom, the yarn and the design is neither shared nor deployed for other orders.

Nathamuni bears the reputation of being extremely responsible (*porruppu*), both with regard to his work and to his word. He is described as prudent in his requests for advances and is valued for his calm, trustworthy (*naaneum murrai*) manner. His status as a leader among Padma Saliyars in Swamimalai is evident from the various village level offices he holds. As *nattanmaikaran* or caste leader, Nathamuni presides over common festivals and life-cycle ceremonies of the eastern subdivision of Padma Saliyar households in Swamimalai. As the secretary of the district-level caste association, however, he represents both divisions and maintains ties beyond his own production network. In the early 70s, when KGR relinquished placing sari orders in Swamimalai, Nathamuni represented Padma Saliyar weaving households in honouring him with a Balakrishna idol in silver purchased from contributions he had mobilised from the community. Again, when a weaver from Swamimalai requires an introduction to a middle-level producer in a neighbouring town, it is Nathamuni who arranges the meeting and mediates between both parties and serves as a guarantor on behalf of the weaver.

Middle Level: Small Producers in Larger Towns

K. G. Ramaswami Chettiar (b. 1935), Kumbakonam, Thanjavur

KGR grew up in a weaving household in T. Pallur near Jayamkondacholapuram in Tiruchirappalli district. There were five looms in their house and together with the products of looms from other households, KGR's uncles (his father died early) Appu Chetti and Perumal Chetti managed a small silk sari business (including the famous silk-cotton mixed Koranadu saris) under the name of Bala Krishna Vilas. By the time he was twenty, KGR along with his older brother K. G. Rengaswami had joined the family business. Bundles of saris woven in their own home as well as those procured from other households in T. Pallur were taken by bus to Kumbakonam, about twenty kilometres away, where they were sold in a rapidly growing market.

In 1950 KGR and his family, including the families of his uncles, moved to Kumbakonam following a market demand for Kanchipuram silk saris. They set up residence in Gandhi

Adigal Street in the vicinity of the prominent Saurashtra silk sari producers in town and sought to expand their own business here. Their main source of production was T. Pallur, where weavers known to them continued to weave saris for them. In 1955 KGR married his sister K. G. Lakshmi to N. Kannan, the son of a micro-level weaver, Narayanaswami Chetti who owned ten looms in Swamimalai. KGR and his brother-in-law N. Kannan soon became partners in business, and KGR slowly gained control of virtually all the looms in Padma Saliyar households in Swamimalai (as shown in Fig. 3.1).

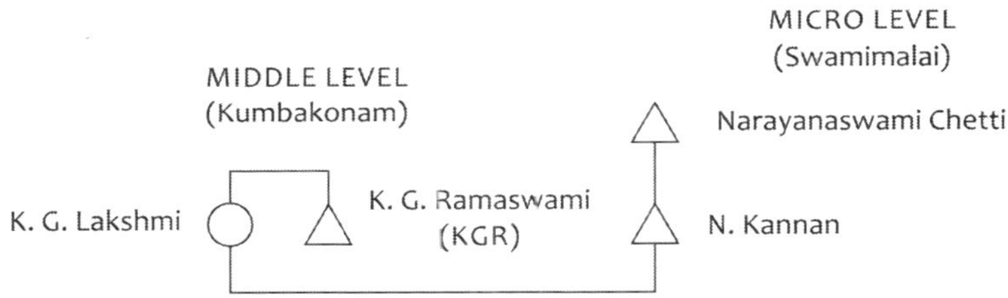

Fig. 3.1: Expansion of loom control through a marriage alliance between middle and micro-level producers.

Source: Author.

After the death of Narayanaswami Chetti in 1972, the partnership between Kannan and KGR also broke up and the looms under their control had to be divided. KGR'S share included looms in his own village, T. Pallur, whereas those in Swamimalai had to be given up as they were in Kannan's native village. KGR lost all control of production in Swamimalai because of the dissolution of the partnership with Kannan.

KGR'S extended kin continue to reside in Gandhi Adigal Street, while KGR and his older brother live in their own house in J. P. Kovil Street, near the Mahamaya Tank.

Their apprenticeships and neighbourly ties with members of the dominant silk weaving Saurashtra community in Kumbakonam buttressed their entry into the field of silk sari production in the state. By 1994, KGR was able to establish fiduciary relations with over five hundred weaving households and build a strong production base.[17] He was able to compete with local Saurashtra silk producers and even gain their admiration as business equals within a single generation through strategic relationships of marriage and business with small-time producers belonging to their own community in Swamimalai and other weaving villages around Kumbakonam.

Organisation of production—from the procurement and preparation of yarn, decisions regarding colours and motifs, to the final stages of folding and packaging—is done entirely in KGR's home under the management and supervision of members of his household. As a wholesale sari producer, KGR prefers to process raw silk yarn before advancing it to weavers. Not only does this guarantee quality standards, it also reduces costs of preparing the yarn outside. Moreover, stocking pre-dyed yarn enables them to tide over fluctuating silk prices, ensuring a stable supply of raw materials and continuous work to weavers throughout the year. The premises are large enough to house a number of hand *charkhas* (spinning wheels) for twisting the raw silk and for dyeing it in copper vats. There is also a separate area for drying the dyed hanks, storing the ready warps in steel cupboards as well as a front room for dealings with weavers (weighing the yarn and gold thread before it is disbursed, computing wages and advances from individual weavers' note-books). The examining of saris for weaving defects and for re-folding and packing them for sale to macro-level businessmen is also done in the same space. The design apparatus, i.e. the bamboo healds (also called heddles) or lifting mechanism in weaving, is ordered from the Lubbai community who specialise in bamboo work and are located in Kumbakonam and its vicinity.

The funds for the wholesale production of saris are also managed by KGR, who is a member of credit societies that organise capital for purchase of raw silk and for giving advances to weavers. He is also a financier in his own right and owns a number of such societies.[18] When he first moved to Kumbakonam in the early 50s, KGR remembers that the competition between silk sari producers in Kumbakonam was so fierce that it had resulted in steep price fluctuations in the market and losses for the entire trade. In 1957, KGR initiated the setting up of the Kumbakonam Handloom Silk Cloth Producer's Association, a body that encouraged active cooperation among middle-level producers who would jointly settle profit margins and sale prices as well as negotiate wages with weavers without undercutting one another. KGR's reputation in the credit market is impressive. According to the manager of the local Karnataka Silk Marketing Board (a government body for supplying wholesale raw silk) under KGR's leadership, silk cloth producers in Kumbakonam have always repaid their loans on time and the Silk Board has not incurred any losses in this town.

Over the years KGR has been successful in winning the trust of a number of weavers in neighbouring villages around Kumbakonam and has gained the reputation of being a successful arbitrator. He has single-handedly settled mutually beneficial negotiations between weavers and merchants on the issue of wages. This is a major accomplishment as, under normal circumstances, amity between owners of capital and those who weave is unthinkable without external, often governmental, mediation. KGR's reputation as one who will not undercut his competitors as well as one responsive to weavers' needs has granted him the unequivocal status of a middle-level leader in Kumbakonam.

KGR has been singularly responsible for activating the state-level Padma Saliyar caste association and donated large sums of money for the economic and social uplift of Padma Saliyars in Tamil Nadu. As president of the Tamil Nadu Padma Saliyar caste association (1999–2004 acting and 2004–2014 elected), KGR has acted on behalf of the community on numerous fronts. He has arranged mass marriages including funding the marriage pendant and wedding saris for the brides, giving textbooks to needy students, setting up schools, instituting scholarships and hosting caste association conferences. His philanthropic activities include building and renovating temples and community marriage halls. KGR built the Shekhar Kalyana Mahal on East J. P. Kovil Street in Kumbakonam and another one in Srirangam. He was responsible for constructing the Anjaneyalu temple in his native village T. Pallur, the Venkatesha Perumal temple in his wife's natal village of Pandruti, and the Bhavanarishi temple on his own street in Kumbakonam for the benefit of his community. His generosity and public presence have gained him and his wife the respect of his community and together they are regularly featured in the caste association's periodical *Padma Saliyar Kural* as respected leaders of the group.

KGR has borne numerous risks under unstable economic policy and market conditions. When the petition against rising rates of raw silk by the Federation of Tamil Nadu Silk Handloom Producers Associations in 2009[19] and again in 2010[20], made to DMK Chief Minister Karunanidhi remained unheeded, KGR led a hunger fast on 25 December 2010[21] and another one on 4 October 2013[22] to mark his protest on behalf of silk handloom weavers and producers in the state. When I met KGR again in 2014, he had suffered a devastating financial loss. Thousands of weavers under his contract had abandoned work and left without paying back their sari advances. Cooperatives, and not private producers, were eligible for the compensation provided to handloom producers by the central government. KGR had been forced to repay the bank loan by selling a large portion of his fixed assets.

Macro Level: Retailers in Big Cities

Nalli Kuppuswami Chetti (b. 1940), Chennai, Tamil Nadu

During the late 1920s when Nalli Kuppuswami's grandfather, Nalli Chinnaswami Chetti travelled to sell silk saris to brahmin customers in Madras, there was just a single loom in their house in Kanchipuram. Open to innovative ideas and taking calculated risks in the business, Kuppuswami's grandfather was the first to adopt chemical dyes for silk yarn in Kanchipuram in the early decades of the twentieth century. In his autobiography *Work is Worship*, Kuppuswami recollects that Chinnaswami encouraged the Swedish chemicals manufacturer Ciba-Geigy to experiment in the family's dye units and to test their suitability for weaving silk saris.[23]

By the time Kuppuswami was twenty years of age, his father and uncles had established the family business of wholesale sari production in Kanchipuram for their customers in Madras. Kuppuswami's marriage to Alamelu, the daughter of middle-level producer S. R. G. Ranganathan Chettiar from Kumbakonam, very early in his career gave a substantial boost to the family concern. Kuppuswami was now in a position to gain access to the products of looms in Kumbakonam. His father-in-law not only commissioned his own looms in Kumbakonam to produce exclusively for Nalli but also handled production for him.

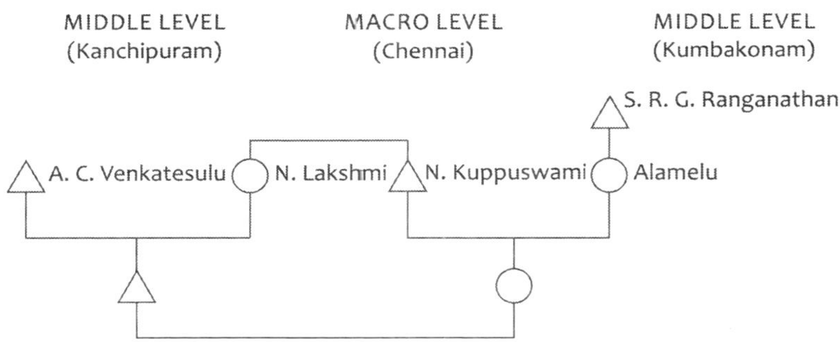

Fig. 3.2: Expansion of loom control through a marriage alliance between macro and middle-level leaders.

Source: Author.

Kuppuswami's sister N. Lakshmi's marriage to middle-level producer and neighbour on Reddipet Street, A. C. Venkatesulu, had also ensured control over a larger number of looms in Kanchipuram. Kuppuswami's control over these looms was further extended when he gave his own daughter, Geetha, in marriage to his nephew (see Fig. 3.2 above).

According to a caste official in Kanchipuram, 'there was a time when no one in Kanchipuram consented to forge marriage alliances with Kumbakonam but since Nalli, this practice has become a norm.' The trans-local partnership has also strengthened the caste association in mobilising members both within Tamil Nadu and beyond. In 1982 Nalli Kuppuswami and his father-in-law S. R. G. Ranganathan Chettiar from Kumbakonam and some other silk leaders, including Chengalvaraya Chettiar of Kumaran Silks from Kanchipuram, were invited to attend the All India Padma Saliyar Association meeting held at Hyderabad. Here nationalist Pragada Kotaiah and other caste leaders from Andhra Pradesh encouraged the delegation to expand the activities of the Tamil Nadu chapter of the caste association.[24] The photograph marking this historic meeting forms the cover page of the second issue of *Padma Jyothi*, the Padma Saliyar community magazine in Telugu brought out from Hyderabad by Pendem Ravindra Rao. Subsequently, Kuppuswami held a meeting at Woodlands Hotel in Madras to re-activate the association and to organise the *Akhil Bharath Padmashali Mahasabha* at T. Nagar in the compound of his home in Panagal Park.

Nalli has been able to mobilise a vast network of kin, affinal and community links, and receives a steady supply of saris from numerous middle-level producers who in turn procure them from over ten thousand looms in silk weaving households in numerous villages in Tamil Nadu. From annual sales of Rs. 2.5 lakhs in the early 30s, by the time Kuppuswami took over in 1961, the business had already grown to INR 28 lakhs (USD 42,000). Since then it multiplied to INR 14 crores (USD 2 million) in 1983 and a decade later, the group's annual sales from all retail outlets in India and abroad were stated to be over INR 110 crores (USD 16 million).

The atmosphere of Nalli's retail showroom in Panagal Park in Chennai reveals a shared sociality and intimate knowledge of silk sari weaving that can only be compared with showrooms of other Padma Saliyar concerns. The counters are ordered according to the value of the sari which in turn refers to the nature of the yarn, i.e. silk or cotton, the density of the pattern and amount of gold wire used. The salesmanship of the male staff also betrays a keen understanding of the colour and design preferences of women patrons. Selected saris are deftly exhibited with patience, unmindful of the number of saris pulled out or the time involved in re-folding them. The entire operation is skilfully orchestrated—there is a particular

Fig. 3.3: Cover page of Telugu newsletter *Padma Jyothi*, 1982, showing Pragada Kotaiah with Nalli Kuppuswami Chetti and other senior members of the caste association in Tamil Nadu, including Chengalvaraya Chettiar of Kumaran Silks and RKR of Radha Silks.

Source: Courtesy, A. S. Krishnamurthy, Chennai; and Srinivas Raj Bairi, President, Padmashali Officials and Professionals' Association (POPA), Hyderabad.

way in which the sari is spread out to reveal its pattern without losing grip over its original fold and without appearing clumsy whilst draping the sari's ornamental end-piece over the left shoulder for the benefit of the customer.

The rapid turnover of stock and the milling crowd at any time in the Nalli showroom is testimony to the popularity of their saris. Kuppuswami admits that their company maintains a policy of low profit margins accompanied by high volume sales. Whereas sari boutiques depend on the uniqueness of their collections advertised as 'handpicked' for discerning, often elite customers, Kuppuswami believes in providing value for money to patrons regardless of their class status and the size of their budget. Nalli is able to reduce prices without compromising the overall design by offering saris with single rather than double borders and by decreasing the amount of gold thread and silk employed. Equally, some of the most expensive wedding saris worth their weight in gold are sold here and customers are made aware of these price-based varieties through bold signs at every counter.

The saris at Nalli are not only distinguished for their price range but also for their quality of being 'pure.' They are guaranteed for their durability and lustre on account of the superiority of the silk used and, as in the case of gold retail, have built a level of trust among their patrons. The dyes are also certified as permanent, particularly because these saris are meant to be washed at home and part of the daily wear of upper caste patrons. Kuppuswami is also transparent about the purity of the zari used in his saris. It is important that wedding saris are 'pure' in all these material aspects in order for them to be auspicious as wedding saris. Nalli and a few other Padma Saliyar retail firms in Chennai like Radha Silks and Kumaran Silks have built their reputation in Chennai as reliable suppliers of 'pure' silk saris.

Kuppuswami likens the bond with his patrons to that of a silk fibre. It is 'a relationship as close and strong as a silk fibre. We are always careful to understand and serve their needs. This is the secret of our trade.'[25] The characteristic tenacity, smooth texture and compact weave of silk yarns provide an apt metaphor for the firm's tight grip over the taste and sensibilities of women customers and the pulse of market trends. Kuppuswami is quick to introduce new colours and combinations (a special range of pastel shades and saris in blacks and whites is reserved for the north Indian market), to vary border widths from very large to small, and to continually offer new motifs (sometimes geometric, at other times figurative) and designs. Sari collections inspired by film stars such as the 'Hema Malini' collection or the 'Kalakshetra' style, mirroring the taste of a classical dancer, are launched to draw attention to contemporary fashion. Complementing their range of Kanchipuram wedding saris, the 'Heritage' collection of traditional silk handloom saris from other states of India is a recent addition.

Nalli's success in the silk handloom sari business is evident from the spread of their producer network, the number of showrooms both in India and abroad, and from their substantial annual sales turnover. Kuppuswami also maintains regional visibility as patron of the arts and religion and holds prominent offices in major cultural academies and temple committees in the city. There is rarely a music or dance performance or temple festival in Chennai which has not been either sponsored or inaugurated by Nalli Kuppuswami. Kuppuswami's competence in judging changing tastes and fashions has also won his saris acclaim in national fashion shows.

Kuppuswami's demonstrated ability to influence decisions in key issues like those of procurement and prices of silk yarn—by securing positions in regional and national governmental bodies like the Tamil Chamber of Commerce and the Central Silk Board—has assured him an influential position in the silk handloom industry. In recognition of his contribution of bringing the work of thousands of weavers in small villages to national and international light, Kuppuswami has been honoured by his fellow caste members with titles like the 'King of Silk' and *Pattu Vanibha Chakravarthi* or 'Emperor of the Silk Trade.' He is recognised as 'The Chettiar' among Padma Saliyar handloom leaders in Tamil Nadu. Indeed, for his community, the Padma Saliyars, Nalli is a 'prodigy,' a man who has done them proud and is eminently worthy of the highest national honour. Kuppuswami was awarded the Padma Shri in 2003 by the Government of India.

WORK: SHARED VALUES AND GOALS

The relations of exchange between the three levels of silk sari production and sale in Tamil Nadu—the procurement of bulk goods by retailers in cities from middle-level producers in towns; the collection of saris by middle-level organisers from weavers; the disbursement of a dyed silk warp for a fresh batch of saris by the producer to the weaver—are characterised by a system of rotating credit. This means that the promise of payment is tied to the promise of a fresh order. It functions within the framework of shared values and the common goal of attaining the status of one worthy of respect (yokkiyamaana) in his/her own domain of work.

Retailers at the city level do not like to keep stock for longer than sixty to ninety days. The shelf life of silk saris is limited, not only because of wear and tear but also because of rapidly changing fashions. Retailers therefore constantly need to renew their stock. There are virtually no immediate cash transfers at this level and payments are made in instalments as and when stocks are consumed. Incentives of discount are built into the ongoing relationship between retailers and wholesalers which enhance profit from sales for the retailer in the city and in turn ensure fresh orders for the wholesaler in the town. At the micro level too, credit is rotated between large sums of money advanced to weavers against an undertaking to weave a batch of saris. Wages are adjusted as saris are completed and another advance is made for the weaving of a new warp of three to six saris.

Such a system of credit is possible only if production occurs within a context that ensures the continuity of ties which have been established on stronger footings than those based on impersonal contracts. 'Being of the same community, people are interested in doing business with us'; 'We prefer to do business with those whom we already know'; 'They need us, we need them, but there must also be trust' are comments frequently made in this regard. We have already seen how carefully selected marriage alliances between levels augment production capacities or strengthen existing ones (see Figures 3.1 and 3.2). Moreover, it is not unusual for seemingly separate and opposed business groups to resolve long-standing rivalries even within the same level. Indeed, caste provides occasion for cooperation within and despite conflict. Kuppuswami of the Nallis group and P. C. Jayaraman of Kumaran Silks were able to transform their generation-long conflict and competition into an enduring business partnership by marrying their children (see Fig. 3.4).

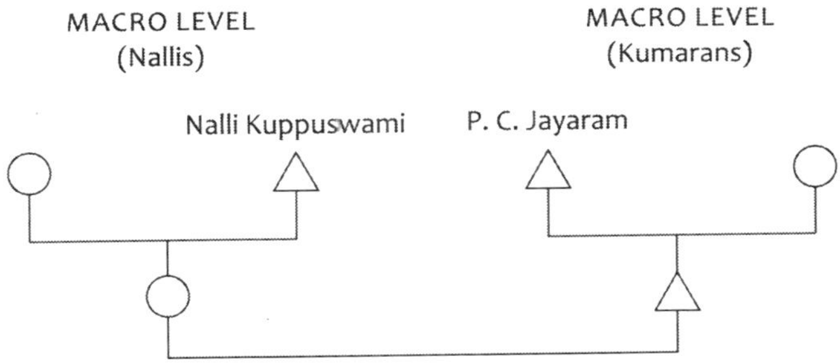

Fig. 3.4: Dissolving business rivalries through a marriage alliance between competitors at the macro level.

Source: Author.

Evidence of such marriage exchanges between competing families belonging to the same level are also common at the middle and micro levels of silk sari production and occur within a code of conduct and ethic that sees conflict and competition as being within the community rather than outside of it.[26]

The potential for mitigating the inequalities and vulnerabilities of production across antagonisms between levels is possible precisely because leadership—on the basis of achieved mastery in one's profession—is recognised and honoured as a common ideal. The potential for such porosity between levels is amply demonstrated in this poem highlighting the shared valence of *nul* for the group. Referring to both the life 'thread' of a weaver and a 'body of knowledge' or 'guide' to ethical living, *Nulum Nulum* is intended as a double entendre by the author and was published in the caste periodical in 1995.[27]

> *Nulum Nulum*
>
> Twisting *kora* [raw silk], straightening the warp, fashioning a life from the loom, balancing its movements to and fro—the daily struggle between that which does

> not come and that which does not go [a reference to the contrasts and ironies of life].
>
> Leaving no work half done, concentrating to ensure not a single thread snaps, imparting beauty to his work by the skill and precision of his hands and the creativity of his mind, the weaver reveals the excellence of his craft.
>
> What he wears is a simple cloth, what he weaves and offers is a silk sari in brilliant gold thread, in crores of designs that arrest the gaze of women.
>
> As he wields the thread (nulum), the day his son reaches out for it (nulum) will be the day the first rays of the sun are immanent and everyone will celebrate his blossoming with fragrance gathered from the eight directions.
>
> So many of our fellow community members, including Nalli Kuppuswami, have risen by wielding the thread (nulum). You too should take to it (nulum) and rise, become accomplished. Step ahead with principles to achieve your goals, and enhance the glory of the Padma Saliyars.

Leadership encodes an ethic of competence in one's work at every level of production in this narration of community values. It upholds hereditary knowledge of weaving as a cultural right and shared norm for the deliverance of justice. The framework of community guarantees that private caste and kin relations and those obtained through public status are not rigidly opposed. Dynamism of production relations is assured within a milieu of cooperative conflicts. The capacity to defend autonomy in one's sphere of work may yet have another basis for contestation and resolution.

ENDNOTES

1. Such a model differs from the macro perspective on handloom production as a sector of the Indian economy. It is also different from that drawn from the more micro-field based caste and village studies in anthropology and adopts a more regionally grounded approach to the vicissitudes of artisan capital in Tamil Nadu. Recently the term non-corporate capital has been used in reference to the historical and

contemporary study of entrepreneurship in Tamil Nadu (Mahadevan and Vijayabaskar 2014).

2. Weaving castes in south India have been recognised as being 'highly differentiated, with some members capable of accumulating capital, and investing it in new production capacity' (Brennig 1990: 86).

3. Arterburn 1982: 128, 134.

4. Bharathan 1985. Saurashtra weaver B. Krishnamurthy, having won a National Award in 2010 for his designs, recalls having been trained under Padma Saliyar weaver-designer Bhupathi for his specialisation in innovative *adai* and *jala* techniques of brocade weaving and who was also featured in the *Frontline* magazine article by Bharathan.

5. In the context of gender asymmetries in household arrangements, Sen argues that both parties gain a lot more by acting in a framework of pervasive cooperation even in instances of direct conflict. He suggests that the 'togetherness' fostered by jointly held household responsibilities in the case of men and women living under the same roof renders conflicts as 'aberrations or deviant behaviour' within an overall format of cooperation (Sen 1987: 42).

6. In her study of the professional community of 'temple dancers' or devadasis in Tamil Nadu, Srinivasan (1988) has shown that gender relations within the *dasi* household were predicated upon wider temple sectarianism and individual professional prestige which legitimised female economic and political authority within it. And even though the men of their caste groups were seen as gurus, the women had relative independence to pursue their unusual lifestyle and professional code and to seek the best possible arrangement for the perpetuation of their art. The household was distinctly matri-centred. Women were not only the primary earners but also managed the daily functioning of the joint household. And even though, technically, both daughters and sons were equal heirs to their mother's income, it was the daughter, and sometimes even an adopted daughter, who actually inherited it.

7. Padma Saliyars spend more at weddings and are increasingly finding matches further afield for greater social mobility and presence in big cities in contrast to the Saurashtras who prefer to give their daughters to friends and neighbours and to have simple wedding ceremonies with shared expenses. Conventionally, marriage links did not extend the borders of Tamil Nadu, and especially not past the town of Gudiyattam, even though some ties were maintained in the neighbouring state of Andhra Pradesh via the caste association.

8. Details of the present organisation of the national-level association are to be found at http://akhilabharatapadmashalisangham.org/contact-us.php

9. The mapping draws from Purushottaman (2005) and Thilakendran (2005) and is intended less as a timeline and more to demonstrate the link between local-level caste associations and caste leaders.

10. My use of the term 'handloom publics' draws from Reddy and Zavos' (2009) concept of 'temple publics' and refers to a complex network of public spheres associated with the Padma Saliyars engaged in silk handloom production in Tamil Nadu and also to the shared spaces in the public life of weavers, producers, retailers, caste association functionaries and diverse intermediaries.

11. Mines 1984: 19.

12. Gorringe has also shown how caste-based mobilisations among groups that have not benefited from Dravidian reform in Tamil Nadu have leadership patterns that are 'analogous to caste headmen' (Gorringe 2010: 121).

13. Equally, honours are actively sought by individuals to establish their pre-eminence in Padma Saliyar society. They underlie the pattern of leadership in south India. See the work of Appadurai 1981; Dickey 1993; Dirks 1987; Fuller 1984; Hardgrave 1979; Mines and Gourishankar 1990; Pandian 1992; Price 1996; and Rudner 1987.

14. This is close to Rudner's discussion of honour among the Nakarattars, a mercantile caste group, where he shows how 'Kumarappan's honours recognized his special role in stimulating and managing the worship and donations of other Nakarattars. In effect, the collective worship at Palani constituted Kumarappan a leader of the Nakarattars and empowered him to act as trustee of all funds donated to the deity' (Rudner 1987: 374).

15. Haynes and Roy 1999; Ludden 1996; Parthasarathi 2001; and Roy 1997.

16. Parthasarathi 2001: 12–13.

17. These included the villages: T. Pallur, Vanathurainpattinam, Chenthurai, Utkottai, Jayamkondacholapuram, Chinthamani, Thirubhuvanam, Papanasam, Ayyampettai, Darasuram, Patteeswaram, Kumbakonam, Karzhuvan Thondi, Valangai Maan, Aaduthurai, Thirumangalam Kudi, Pandruti and Mannargudi.

18. Srinivasa Chits and Finance, Srinivasa Investments, Kudanthai Lakshmi Srinivasa Chits Pvt. Ltd and Sri Srinivasa Chits were the credit societies owned by KGR at the time of the commencement of my research.

19. 'Kumbakonam silk weavers spin a tale of woes,' U. Bharath, *The Indian Express*, Kumbakonam, 31 December 2009. http://www.newindianexpress.com/states/tamil_nadu/article88981.ece

20. 'Federation seeks raw silk at 50 per cent subsidy,' Special Correspondent, *The Hindu*, Thanjavur, 21 November 2010. http://www.thehindu.com/todays-paper/tp-national/tp-tamilnadu/federation-seeks-raw-silk-at-50-per-cent-subsidy/article903165.ece

21. In an interview with KGR cited in the *Padma Saliyar Kural*.

22. 'Weavers demand raw silk at low price, hold fast,' by Special Correspondent, *The Hindu*, 4 October 2013. http://www.thehindu.com/todays-paper/tp-national/tp-tamilnadu/weavers-demand-raw-silk-at-low-price-hold-fast/article5199174.ece

23. Kuppuswami [1983] 2004: 21–2.

24. The ground work for Kuppuswami's leadership role in the community had already begun in 1952 when his father Narayanaswami Chetti along with other community leaders had felicitated Padma Saliyar handloom activist and MLA Pragada Kotaiah at the Woodlands Hotel, Madras, to discuss the condition of the handloom industry and to raise political awareness among them.

25. Kuppuswami 1983: 35.

26. Community-based division of labour such as this, it must be emphasised, is distinct from the 'moral economy' of peasant households where social and moral arrangements ensure subsistence often at the cost of autonomy and status (cf. Scott 1976). It also contrasts with Banaras, where *katauti* or illegal and arbitrary deductions are made by producers belonging to other communities (Kumar 1988: 44).

27. Gopalaswami 1995: 15. I am grateful to S. Gopalaswami for giving us permission to translate his poem for this volume; and to V. Sujatha and L. Kannan for this translation of the poem, which is not true to the original poetic form and attempts to merely grasp the poem's essence.

FOUR

WEAVING AS SACRAMENT

In late February of 2012, the Kanchipuram division of the Tamil Nadu Padma Saliyar association invited me to attend the *kodi utsavam* or flag hoisting ceremony held on the first day of a ten-day festival at the Kamakshiamman temple. The right (*urimai*) to sponsor the cloth for the temple flag at this festival is held by the family of D. Babu, the manager of the Nalli showroom at Chennai; he and his wife Hamsa were the *ubhayakarans* or patrons at the event. A dispute between a brahmin family and D. Babu's grandfather some seventy-five years ago is said to have been resolved in favour of the latter and restored the Padma Saliyars' right to public honours at this temple. Members of the community are said to have 'proved' the legitimacy of their claim on the basis of their caste-puranas and gained the privilege of offering the flag cloth and receiving the *kovil mariyaathai* or temple honours in the presence of the deity.

The ceremony took place in the inner sanctum where an officiating priest bestowed D. Babu with a silken head cloth in recognition of his family's links with the temple. This was followed by the ritual being repeated for office bearers of each subdivision of the Tamil Nadu Padma Saliyar association present. A functionary of the Kanchipuram chapter of the association called out their names one by one (using the Telugu term *peddanakar* rather than the Tamil *nattanmaikaran*) as they received the symbolic honour with flower garlands in the inner sanctum. The ceremony was repeated outside in the pillared courtyard of the temple precinct (see Fig. 4.1), where members of the congregation received shawls and leaf-packed lunch packets of flavoured rice.

Fig. 4.1: A meeting of the Tamil Nadu Padma Saliyar Sangam being conducted by the Kanchipuram chapter of the caste association in the precinct of the Kamakshiamman temple after representatives of the different chapters received ritual honours in the presence of the deity in February 2012.

Source: Courtesy the photographer, Rags Raghavan.

The local caste association's president Dr. Sumati Ayyah along with secretary N. Babu urged community members to pay the annual fee and to regularly attend its meetings and functions. They spoke of caste matters—of ethical values pertaining to life and work and of the 'record' of the Padma Saliyars' involvement in the calendric events of this temple of goddess Kamakshi—made possible through the initiative and efforts of the sangam.

The enactment of collective honour at a major temple in Kanchipuram endorses caste privilege at the regional level for the many small and big Padma Saliyar leaders in a landscape of multiple hierarchies in Tamil Nadu. Honour and redistribution at public rituals have historically been a means of social mobility for many lower ranking groups in the caste hierarchy in south India. The rise of temple towns in the medieval period was in fact associated with the growing economic prosperity and social mobility of weavers among other artisans.[1] By the middle of the fourteenth century, temples in south India had become the loci of intense sectarian activity and it was through public ritual and acts of authority, honour and redistribution that enabled groups ranked within the fourth *varna* or caste to be absorbed into the ambit of Sanskritic Hinduism. The role of weavers in expanding markets and the growing importance given to them by kings, especially later during the Vijayanagar period in the fifteenth to sixteenth centuries, saw weaving communities claiming a higher caste status. The division of the fourth varna into *shudras* and the superior *sat shudras* is part of this increasing caste differentiation in society.[2]

Distinction amidst competing groups in the caste hierarchy was guaranteed during periods of heterodoxy and engagement with the discourse of Puranic brahminism. It was at such times that claims of cosmic sanction were canonised as myths of origin within the caste-puranas. Caste-puranas are valuable in unveiling the diverse motives that impel their articulation and re-articulation. They are tools of caste legitimacy in establishing or contesting a particular claim in the presence of a mediating authority. The conscious defiance or fallen status in the mythic narrative of a particular caste underscores conflicting status claims rather than actual events in the history of a group. The preface to the *Devanga Purana*, the mythic text of the Devanga caste of hereditary weavers in the Tamil region, for instance, describes the exact context in which the Purana was used by the caste group. According to Das (1982), the translation of the text from the original Sanskrit into Tamil took place under the auspices of a local landlord who had the power to settle disputes within his domain of influence and issued a charter of legitimacy for their claim to a higher caste rank.[3]

Caste-puranas enunciate a group's self-perception, religious and/or local identity, aspirations for upward mobility and professional specialisation. They offer 'evidence' of status in the caste hierarchy, of privileges accrued and/or dwindled through genealogy and represented in the extended story of descent and migration. The mythic text of the Padma Saliyars establishes their collective lineage to the higher gods of Sanskritic Hinduism. It chronicles their sectarian affiliation, not only by establishing their ancestry to sage Markandeya but also by asserting their singularity as 'original' weavers or those who wove for the gods. Vishnu is said to have provided the Padma Saliyars with thread and Shiva with colour, legitimating their claim to temple honours and privileges in regionally significant vaishnava and shaiva temples.

The emergence of the *Bhavanarishi Puranam* as a significant text in the body of caste literature of the Padma Saliyars in the twentieth century is not clear.[4] The preface indicates that the translation from the Sanskrit original was done by *bhaagavathar* Azhagirisami Chettiar and overseen by Tamil scholar Subbarama Ayyar of Native College, Madurai, in 1905. Even though the exact context of its translation is not provided, colonial census enumerations, ethnographic projects and craft surveys may have been an impetus. This was also the period which saw the economic growth of Madurai town, a phenomenon coincident with the ascendency of Saurashtra merchants and silk weavers in the region at the time.[5] Increasing differentiation of the weaving population now spread out over clusters of small towns could have been a source of rivalry and competition among weaving groups.[6] The Saurashtras and

Padma Saliyars are the dominant weaving castes in the region and acknowledge one another as equals. The *Saurashtra Mani,* the journal of the Saurashtras brought out from Kumbakonam, for instance, paid tribute to silk producer KGR by placing his image on the front cover in 2004. Again, in the 2010 edition of the *Bhavanarishi Puranam*, the preface has been written by a Saurashtrian scholar. Nevertheless, the fact that the caste-purana was first translated and published in Madurai, as were the second (1987) and third (2010) editions, is strongly suggestive of Padma Saliyar caste assertion in the region.

Fig. 4.2: The second (1987) and third (2010) editions of the *Bhavanarishi Puranam* in Tamil. The original translation was done by B. A. Chettiar in 1905 and published from Native College, Madurai.

Source: Courtesy, C. Thirumalai Chettiar (heir of B. A. Chettiar).

The different editions provide access to the motives underpinning their publication and offer insights into the context of their use. For instance, the second edition was published under the sponsorship of Padma Saliyar silk leader S. R. G. Ranganathan Chettiar from Kumbakonam while the third edition was produced with donations from KGR from Kumbakonam by Padma Saliyar preceptor C. Thirumalai, the *dharmakarta* of the Bhavanarishi temple at Avaniyapuram since 1974. The image on the back cover of the latest edition features the Bhavanarishi temple in Avaniyapuram on the day of the *kumbabishekam* or consecration in the year 2005. Supra-local leadership as an organising principle of community is reiterated here in the case of the circulation (through free distribution among caste fellows) of the caste-purana as a text of shared ethics.

The opening pages of each edition feature photographs of silk leaders marking their continued patronage of caste ties through notes of caste exaltation, stressing the Purana's significance to the material and moral well-being of the community. The Purana aims to surpass the local caste order and its hierarchical ranking through its appeal to spiritual and ethical categories taken from the *varna-ashrama-dharma* scheme in Hinduism.[7] The *Bhavanarishi Puranam* articulates shared pride and self-respect whilst simultaneously being prescriptive of beliefs and practices appropriate for the person-in-the-world. Reading and enacting the Puranas can imbue an individual or a group with 'puranic mentality' such that even as one immerses oneself in the spiritual or the metaphysical, one is '... always fully merged in worldly life.'[8] Descriptions of worldly agents, both human and animal, events, know-how and geographies in conjunction with spiritual beings and sacred paraphernalia make the implausible plausible in the legends of the Puranas. Puranic spatio-temporality is superimposed upon human space and time so that its subscribers may identify with and indeed dissolve distinctions between the manifest here and now and the unmanifest then and there of earthly existence. In the proceeding section, I examine myths drawn from the *Bhavanarishi Puranam* that validate the Padma Saliyars as weavers of cloth for gods of the Hindu pantheon.[9]

DIVINE ORIGIN: WEAVERS OF CLOTH FOR GODS AND HUMANS

The *Bhavanarishi Puranam* establishes a genealogical link between the Padma Saliyars and the high gods of medieval Hinduism—Brahma, Vishnu and Shiva. Not only that, the various myths recount weaving as a cosmic bequest linked to a large body of knowledge received from these gods by the Padma Saliyars' immediate ancestor and caste deity Bhava Narayana or Bhavanarishi. Padma Saliyars adhering to the vaishnava sectarian affiliation refer to their mythical progenitor as 'Bhava' Narayana or the image of Narayana, referring to Vishnu himself, whereas the shaiva Padma Saliyars refer to him as Bhavanarishi. This sectarian differentiation of the community, however, does not restrict intermarriage so that in one family there may be adherents of both. Generally, it is followed along the male line. This is consonant with their mythology and ritual life in which both Vishnu and Shiva figure as important deities. The Purana narrative outlines the birth of Bhavanarishi or Bhava Narayana from the sacred fire bearing the knowledge of weaving which is then passed on to the original Padma Saliyars for use in the making of cloth, initially for the gods, and eventually for humans.

Cosmic Lineage: Myth 1

In the beginning, at the time of cosmic regeneration, gods and humans are both created without any covering for their bodies. In a large celestial *sabhai* or assembly, the Holy Trinity and the many lesser *devas* or celestial beings sit down to discuss the problem of shielding their nudity and self-respect or honour. They agree to seek the help of Markandeya, who had been granted the boon of immortality by Shiva himself. Markandeya was at that time engrossed in performing the *putra kameshti yagna* or the 'fire sacrifice for the birth of a son.'

Through the power of his invocations and in presence of all the gods, Markandeya conceives a being whose figure arises from the flames of the *homa kundam* or sacrificial pit. With the likeness (*amaippu*) of Narayana (another name for Vishnu), the divine offspring of Markandeya is striking in appearance. His handsome body adorned with *aayuthams* or weapons and implements shines with a youthful glow while his hair, the colour of the *navaratna* or nine gems, gleams like sunbeams (*kodi suryaprakasam*). Created from the power of the five *mantras* or chants in the image of Narayana, Bhava Narayana comes to be known as *pancha bhuthi* or one born from the five elements. He embodies within him the divine knowledge and skill of weaving cloth and proposes to resolve the problem of honour for all present. Awestruck by the force of the *jnanam udaiyam* or divine generation of knowledge, the celestial gathering inquires as to how Bhava Narayana intended to produce the cloth so required. In response, Bhava Narayana offers to create the loom upon which the cloth could be woven. He undertakes the creation of the loom from his own body: from his head appears the cloth beam; from his arms the vertical pillars that hold the weaving frame together; from his chest are made the healds or heddles, the warp separating mechanisms; his spine forms the overhead horizontal bar of the loom frame; and lastly, from his legs and feet come the foot pedals or treadles. In another version of the myth, Bhavanarishi kills the demon Kaaluvasuran and takes his skull, intestines, bones, nerves and other body parts and gives them to the Padma Saliyars to fashion tools for *karuvighal* or weaving.

The fibres reeled out from the stem of the lotus emerging from Vishnu's *undhi kammalam* or navel form the yarn required for weaving the cloth. Markandeya himself winds this *padma nul* or thread around his crossed knees and gives it to his son Bhava Narayana to commence weaving.[10] With the help of secret instructions on the technique of weaving in the *sambavi mantram* granted to him by Brahma, Bhava Narayana proceeds to produce lotus fibre cloth that is as white and shimmering as the petals of Vishnu's lotus.

Bhava Narayana is now able to offer the gods and devas each a cloth to cover their nudity and regain their honour. For Vishnu, the *pitaambaram*; a 'narayana bordered' cloth for goddess Lakshmi; for Vishnu's vehicle Garuda, the Garuda *dhwaja* or flag; the *saalvai* or cloth of honour for Brahma; a *pushpa vastram* or flower cloth for goddess Saraswati; 'creeper bordered' cloths for Rati and Manamada; and so on for all the thirty-three crore (ten million) gods. The entire assembly is now illuminated (*prakaashitam*) with the radiance and lustre of the *punya vastras* or sacred cloths woven by Bhava Narayana. In admiration, the gods liken the glow to the brilliance of the *navaratna* or nine gems and bestow upon Bhavana the title of *maana rakshaka* or guardian of honour and *maanathey kathavar* or bearer of self-respect. This deed, that is the creation of clothes to cover the nudity of gods and men, confers upon Bhavana the status of one equal only to Brahma, the creator of humans and this world. Brahma now blesses him and announces that he is in fact a member of his own clan.

Having provided cloths woven of lotus fibre to all, Bhavanarishi approaches Shiva who wore only tiger skin. He beseeches Shiva to wear the cloth woven by him in order for his mission to be fulfilled. Shiva concedes to take Bhavana's *divya vastra* as a flag adorning his vehicle Hrishaba, the bull, and calls it the 'Hrishaba Dhuvajan.' He blesses Bhavanarishi and decrees that in all the *sthalas* or territories (temples) where Shiva is worshipped, the cloth woven by Bhavana shall be used as the *thiruvizha kodi* or festival flag during the *kodi utsavam* or flag hoisting ceremony. Shiva further proclaims that the descendants of Bhavanarishi will have the primary right to offer the cloth flag of Shiva at these temples.

Later in the narrative, Bhavanarishi marries Bhadravati, the daughter of Surya the sun god and Chhayadevi or goddess shadow, who bears him a hundred and one sons.[11] Bhavanarishi performs their *upanayaanam* or sacred thread ceremony, teaches them the four *vedas*, six *shastras* and thirty-two *dharmas* and the *sambavi mantram* for the knowledge and skill of creating fine cloths for the gods. Of these sons, one hundred became the forefathers of the Padma Saliyars while the remaining son is the ancestor of the Pattu (silk) Saliyars. The two do not intermarry and both have vaishnava and shaiva divisions as well as a number of exogamous sects.

Bhavanarishi then takes his hundred and one sons to Narayana, and says, 'Oh *lokarakshaka*, preserver of this world, I made cloth with the fibres drawn from the lotus stem emerging from your navel and gained the title of *maana rakshakan* with your blessings. I now present to you my sons. Bless them as your servants (*Maha Vishnu dasai*) and make this occupation theirs.' Vishnu goes on to present each son of Bhavanarishi with a seed from the lotus. 'Upon sowing these seeds in the earth,' Vishnu explains, 'a *parutti chedi* (cotton plant) will grow which, when ripe, will split and yield a substance as white as my *shankha* (conch).' The sons of Bhavana are then instructed by Shiva on how to draw this material of greater density into yarn. 'In the *Treta yuga*,' Shiva explains, 'you will use your sharp eyes (*kannu parvaiyaalum*) to weave this yarn into cloth; in the *Dwapara yuga*, through the power of your words (*vaakkaalum*) you shall create wondrous cloths; and in the *Kali yuga*, you shall use your hands to produce cloth.[12] You will offer these cloths to both gods and humans (*devar maanavarghal*) who will in turn give you, the Padma Salis, due respect and thus you will live in wealth and prosperity.'

At this juncture the Padma Saliyars present Shiva with a question and ask, 'Why do you want us to draw cotton thread rather than lotus thread?' Shiva smiles at the grandchildren of Markandeya and says, 'My obedient students, in every *yuga*, due to indiscipline and faithlessness in the Vedas, rulers and their subjects will be dissatisfied with the qualities and merits of lotus thread for their future generations. They will prefer what they feel is more impervious material for weaving compared to the lotus fibre which yields a somewhat diaphanous cloth.' The myth goes on to say that in the present era, humans and gods (in their shrines) require cloth that is dense, rather than sheer, in order to cover their nudity. Satisfied thus and equipped with the *sambavi mantram* for weaving fine cloth, the Padma Saliyars return to their home in Kannakathiripura to weave clothes for both gods and humans and prosper by their cosmically ordained weaving profession.

The Padma Saliyars say that they belong to the clan (*vamsham/gothram*) of Markandeya, whose ancestry can be traced via Bhavanarishi to sage Bhrigu, Dhata, Mrikandu, Markandeya, and forms an integral part of their caste literature, both oral and textual, and links them to the high gods of Sanskritic Hinduism.

Fig. 4.3: *Shri Bhrigu Padma Saliya Vamsha Vriksham* or the 'Padma Saliya Genealogical Tree' depicting the 101 sons of Bhavanarishi and goddess Bhadravati.

Source: *Makarishi Markandeya Rishi Charitai* (Chennakrishnan 1980: 7). Courtesy, Tamil Nadu Padma Saliyar Sangam, Chennai.

A myth of origin collected by colonial ethnographer Edgar Thurston in the Baramahal Records of the Madras Presidency, Section III on Inhabitants (1907), narrates how the Padma Saliyars believe they gained their unique distinction as weavers of cloth for the gods.

Cosmic Lineage: Myth 2

The story refers to the time when the annual ritual of presenting a piece of cloth to Markandeya rishi was in the hands of other weaver sects. One year when they failed to make their offering within the customary period, the enraged rishi performed a *yagya* or fire sacrifice and, by the power of his mantras, caused a man to spring from its flames. He named him Padma Saliwarlu and instructed him to produce cloth for his use. This he did and presented the woven material to the rishi saying, 'Oh Swami, who is thy servant to worship, and how is he to obtain *moksham* or admittance to the presence of the Supreme?' The rishi answered, 'Pay adoration to me, and thou wilt obtain *moksham*.'[13]

The Padma Saliyars believe that they are in possession of the skill for weaving fine cloths on account of being the offspring of the union of light and shadow (the very source of the visible world of colour and sensation) on both sides. On the maternal side, as noted earlier, they are the descendants of the source of light, the sun, and shadow, Chhayadevi. On the paternal side they trace their ancestry to Bhrigu (born from the luminous skin of Brahma) and Khyathi whose father, Kardama, was born from the shadow of Brahma's body.

The significance of light and shadow in weaving has been pointed out by Mehta (1992) among Muslim weavers of Barabanki in north India for whom even white is a 'colour' born of the distinction between light and dark. By specialising in weaving the sacred white shroud for their community, the Ansari is said to achieve the status of a *nurbaft* or 'weaver of (white) light' itself. In the case of the Padma Saliyars we have already seen that the lotus yarn used by Bhavanarishi to weave cloth for the gods was translucent, a source of light (and shadow). The cloths woven by this thread caused the entire celestial assembly to be illuminated with their chromatic brilliance (Myth 1). But with the coming of Kali yuga, the need arose for a more impervious cloth which would cover nudity. Moreover, in this era the powers of producing sheer cloth were limited to what was humanly possible, i.e. with the skill of one's hands and not through the power of sight (eyes) and sound (words; Myth 1). At this point, light and dark (sun and shadow) unite to produce matter/colour for the use, more specifically, of humans. Taken together, the two myths establish the divine sanction given to the Padma Saliyars to move from weaving diaphanous cloths (from luminous lotus fibre) for the gods to cloths of greater density (like cotton) for humans in the course of the four eras.

This move from nature to culture, divine to human, described in the mythic narrative below, is further validated by the Padma Saliyar's genealogical link to goddess Bhadravati who is born of the union of light and shadow. Indeed, her marriage with Bhavanarishi establishes the basis for their self-representation as weavers of light in the cosmic world, and of colour (matter) in the human, and commences with an original sin.

Marriage of Bhavanarishi: Myth 3

The Padma Saliyars believe that the first cloth (even a small piece) woven on a new loom must never be worn or discarded. Instead, it is venerated as a sacred offering of the loom and typically remains on the loom. So that when Bhavanarishi presents a fruit of the loom to Shiva, he refuses to accept the gift of cloth as it is not the *first* offering of the loom. Insulted, Shiva curses Bhavanarishi that in future all cloths woven by him would last for no more than six months. Bhavanarishi begs forgiveness and asks if he could seek redress for his mistake in any way, at which point Shiva decrees that redemption would be possible only if Bhavanarishi procures a tiger's skin for Shiva instead. Narada, the celestial mediator comes to Bhavanarishi's assistance and guides him to the forests of

Mount Udayagiri where Bhadravati, the daughter of Surya alone can help him procure the skin of a tiger to appease the wrath of Shiva.

Meanwhile, Bhadravati was aware of Bhavanarishi's prowess in weaving fine cloths. She had also heard of his divine birth as a *divya purusha* from her father, Surya, who had once shown her a cloth woven by Bhavana. Fascinated by the magnificence of the cloth, Bhadravati resolves to seek the creator of such perfection. Tipped off by mischievous Narada, she rounds up all the tigers in the very place that Bhavanarishi is hunting and orders her companions to usher him to her upon arrival. Dressed in the likeness of a goddess and seated on a throne decorated by flower garlands, Bhadravati enchants Bhavanarishi by her resplendent charm. She proposes to assist him in the task of capturing a tiger on condition that he take her hand in marriage. To this Bhavanarishi consents and is now in a position to use the tiger as his *vaahanam* or vehicle to reach the abode of Shiva, Mount Kailasam. Shiva tears open the tiger with his bare nails (in the myth described by Thurston 1909, Vol. 5, Shiva's holy ashes cause the tiger to shed its skin) and removes the skin for himself. In this myth, not only is the dichotomy between skin (for Shiva) and cloth (for humans) made amply clear but also, Bhavanarishi's ability to woo/ tame nature (Bhadravati of the forest) is directly linked to his cultural skill—weaving cloth.

The wedding of Bhavanarishi and goddess Bhadravati is described in great detail in the *Bhavanarishi Puranam*. It narrates how the event was organised in full splendour and attended by all the gods and devas. The myth relates how the couple receive the blessings of all present including the sons of Surya, Yama and Shani who are also now related to the Padma Saliyars as the brothers of Bhadravati. Yama, the god of death, grants the Padma Saliyars immortality and a place in the heavenly resting place of Vishnu or *vaikuntha*. Shani, the lord of Saturn, promises not to present obstacles before them. Thus protected and favoured with a cosmic lineage, the Padma Saliyars revere the divine couple as their caste deities.

Bhavanarishi commands his hundred and one sons and their progeny to worship him together with his consort in a temple especially devoted to them, to perform various rituals and festivals (*utsavams*) and gain their blessings for everlasting prosperity in their occupation. To this day, the Padma Saliyars worship their community deities, Bhavanarishi and Bhadravati, in local shrines especially dedicated to them. The tiger, their vehicle, continues to be held in reverence by them and forms the emblem of their community flag.

SAFEGUARDING A COSMIC RIGHT TO WEAVING

Temple Rights: Myth 4

The Padma Saliyars' cosmic genealogy legitimises the group's links to major shrines of Vishnu and Shiva in Tamil Nadu. At the Uppiliappan *kovil*, a vaishnava temple in Kumbakonam, Thanjavur district, the main deity, Vishnu as Uppiliappan, is depicted together with Markandeya (mythic ancestor of the Padma Saliyars). The *sthala purana* or territorial legend of the temple testifies to Markandaya's relationship to Vishnu as that of a father-in-law and serves as a backdrop to the Padma Saliyar claim and self-identity as descendants of Markandeya rishi and, by the same token, affines of Vishnu.

According to the legend of Uppiliappan at Kumbakonam, sage Markandeya once performed severe penance in a forest beneath the *tulasi* or holy basil plant in order to gain the favour of Vishnu. Pleased by his devotion, Vishnu promises to visit Markandeya but in the meantime is said to have directed goddess Lakshmi to go to Markandeya as a child on his behalf. Finding a girl child beneath the tulasi plant, Markandeya is pleased to gain a daughter and fosters her as a parent. Later, in the month of *Panguni* (March–April), on the lunar day of *ekadasi* when the *thiruonam* asterism is ascendant, Vishnu appears before Markandeya in the guise of a rishi and asks for the hand of his daughter, Bhumidevi, in marriage. Markandeya pleads that she is too young and inexperienced even to know how much salt to put in his food. Amused by Markandeya's dilemma, Vishnu appears before him in his true form and pronounces that he will marry the daughter of Markandeya in this shrine in the month of *Aippasi* (October–November). Vishnu further grants that the forest be henceforth known as Markandeya Kshetram and Tulasivanam and ordains that the place be known as Tiruvinnagaram after his abode in vaikuntham or the temple shrine of Tirupati in present day Andhra Pradesh.[14]

Temple complexes have been the nuclei of urban growth, and inscriptions from the medieval period in south India testify to the role of weavers and cloth merchants in this expansion. The genesis of the town of Tirupati was, according to Ramaswamy (1985), the result of the building of the temple of Vishnu as Venkateswara in the twelfth century and royal patronage and the expansion of trade and commerce later under the Vijayanagar kings. The Padma Saliyars cite inscriptional evidence from this period to defend their extant right to ritual and honour at major vaishnava shrines in the region.

In the late 1980s, the then president of the Tirupati Padmasali Welfare Association, M. V. Ramanaiah circulated a small booklet titled 'Evidence Vouchsafed by Goddess Padmavathi of Thiruchanur in Favour of the Padmsalis' at a meeting held at Tirupati in which a number of prominent members of the Tamil Nadu Padma Saliyar caste association were present. The booklet compiled in English asserts the *Mackenzie Manuscripts* as its original source and refers to an actual gift-deed inscribed on a copper plate in the possession of Tirupati Tirumala Devasthanam Trust. I quote below its contents to show how colonial records of inscriptions are used to defend the right of the Padma Saliyars to offer *seer varasai* or ritual offerings made by affines at the annual enactment of the marriage ceremony of Vishnu with goddess Lakshmi, whom they refer to as 'our daughter' (*namma veedu ponnu*).

> "There was a dispute between the Padmasalis and the Jandras (Devanga caste of weavers). Each community claimed Lakshmi Devi (consort of Vishnu) as the daughter belonging to its own house. They took the dispute to the then ruling king Purushotattama Rayalu. He decided that

> the fit person to settle such a dispute was Chinnanna, grandson of Annamacharya and therefore invited him to his court. Chinnanna took the king Purushottama Rayalu, Tirumala Tatacharyulu, the Jandras and the Padmasalis to the temple of Alamelumangamma. He invoked the Goddess and made Herself to say to which of the above two communities she really belonged. All were astonished to see that the stone-image of the Goddess spoke in a human voice" to pronounce that she belonged to the *vamsham* or clan of the Padma Salis.[15]

The booklet goes on to describe how in the year 1541 (1463 according to the Telugu calendar year, *salivahana saka*) the ancestors of the Padma Saliyars presented a copper plate *dana patrika* or gift deed (once located at the southern *mandapam* of the Padmavathi temple at Tiruchanur) to Tallapakka Chinnanna, declaring that the descendants of Bhavanarishi and Bhadravati, the in-laws of Vishnu, and the grandchildren of Surya on the maternal side and of Brahma from the paternal side, the Padma Shalis of Markandeya *gothram*, spread over fifty-six countries and well versed in *upanayaanam* and *sandhya vandanam,* were granted titles, ornaments, headgear and ceremonial praise, and their work was henceforth uplifted.

The Padma Saliyars' cosmic genealogy offers them demonstrable links to major temples in Tamil Nadu and grants them the elevated status of 'original' weavers of cloth for the gods. Indeed, their mythology describes how others who have tried to usurp this 'art of gaining self-respect' (*mana rakshaka viddhe*) using unfair means have been vanquished in the past by Bhavanarishi, who continues to safeguard the interests of his descendants even today.

Many legends in the Purana describe Bhavanarishi as being accomplished in warfare. He is, however, portrayed as combative only with regard to his role in protecting both the received knowledge of weaving and his progeny from outside threats. This is in contrast to Murugan, the caste deity of the Tamil-speaking Kaikkolar weavers who, according to Mines (1984) is chiefly associated with hunting and to whom the nine original Kaikkolars are said to have offered their services as warriors and therefore not exclusively associated with the weaving profession. Late eighteenth-century scroll paintings depicting the life and heroic deeds of Bhavanarishi and attributed to the *Markandeya Purana* have been found from the Telangana region.[16] Bhavanarishi is depicted as a guardian of the cosmically received knowledge of weaving by the Padma Saliyars and helps them retrieve it from envious adversaries in one encounter in the cosmic battlefield described in a mythic narrative below.

Subduing Rivals and Opponents: Myth 5

One day when the Padma Saliyars are on their usual rounds distributing cloths with beautiful *chitram* or designs to devas in their celestial abode, the nephews of the demon Kaaluvasuran, in their search for new inventions (*adishayangal*), witness the exchange invisibly. Awestruck by the cosmic brilliance (*divya tejovanthargal*) of the clothes and of those wearing them, they become desirous of the knowledge of creating such fine raiment. They approach their uncle Kaaluvasuran for assistance in obtaining the secret mantram or chant from the Padma Saliyars, which they are eventually able to steal through their guile (*thrittuthanamaha*). A fight then ensues in which Bhavanarishi comes to the rescue of his sons and vanquishes Kaaluvasuran and his nephews with the help of *varams* or boons and the many *divya astram* or cosmic weapons granted to him by Shiva.

The Padma Saliyars recount these myths to claim the celestial antecedents of their occupation and to uphold their primal links to the weaving profession. As descendants of Bhavanarishi, who wove cloth from lotus stem fibres, the Padma Saliyars attribute their caste name to this relation with the *padma* or lotus emanating from Vishnu's navel and *shali* from the Sanskrit *shaalika* meaning weaver. In another interpretation, the word *shali* refers to the Sanskrit word meaning beholder of received knowledge or intelligence. Their divine origin as described in their caste-purana sets them apart as weavers of cloth for the gods, legitimising their entitlement to social and ritual honour in the world of humans.

Spatialising Community through Sectarian Ritual Practice

The social bifurcation along the *idangai* or 'left-hand' and the *valangai* or 'right-hand' divisions since the Chola period has been seen to be the matrix for the expression of rivalries and disputes between those of the same occupation in south India.[17] In the context of caste disputes over status ranking and honours conferred under the aegis of regionally significant temples, Price (1991) makes a distinction between 'acting in public' and 'forming a public.' She notes that under the influence of colonial rule, publically sanctioned rituals that once articulated political relations between right and left-hand castes also became the loci for collective action among horizontally constituted supra-local groups, giving greater credence to issues of caste identity. Caste-based work identities are also rendered visible through religious assertions countering brahminical orthodoxy.

The symbolic representations of sectarian groups, enunciated and performed at periodic rituals and ceremonies, have very concrete rewards for the group in question. And contrary to Dumont's (1970) presumed separation between the metaphysical and the material in the conceptual ordering of caste, 'the actual rankings of caste take variable forms in space (regional caste systems) and in time (caste mobility).' The countless measures of identity practices emphasising subtle differences among caste groups, as Chatterjee (1989) has shown among the middle rungs of the caste hierarchy in eighteenth-century Bengal, demonstrate the 'varying strategies of survival, and of self-assertion' of minor sects under conditions of subalternity.[18]

Sectarian movements among the lower ranked shudra castes have sought to deviate from orthodox brahminical norms and prescribed paths for the common goal of *moksha* or liberation not only for the renouncer but also for the person-in-the-world engaged in vital practical activity.[19] According to Thapar, *sannyasa* (and the *ashrama* doctrine or 'four stages of life' in general) was offered to the individual brahmin as an optional fourth stage in an effort to contain these sectarian movements so that caste could be maintained and dissent made less apparent.[20] The Padma Saliyar's choice of religious practice—sacrifice or ritualised abnegation—is an expression of heterodox resistance to domination and subordination in the pursuit of concrete, material ends in-this-world.

The term 'sacrifice' in anthropological literature refers to a variety of ritual complexes such as offerings of first fruits to deities and expiation through vows of abstention. In her examination of the religious life of the Tamil Kaikkolar weavers, Reiniche (1987) observes that 'total devotion (*bhakti*) is self-surrender equivalent to self-sacrifice at the mythical and ritual levels.'[21] In its most general aspect, sacrifice is a sacrament comprising a union of the sacred with the profane. Typically, it entails: i) a separation from normal life in preparation for communion with the divine; ii) the entry into, and contact with, the domain of the sacred; and iii) a renewed admission into the mundane world.[22]

We have seen how at the mythic level Padma Saliyar identity is constituted in the cosmic realm through their genealogy and celestially ordained skill as weavers of fine raiment. In ritual life, shared identity as professional weavers emerges from their identification with, and participation in, sacrificial religion at the regional, street and household levels. The daily practice and ethics of weaving as sacrifice comes together in-this-world through publically sanctioned ritual performances at different spatial levels that function to proclaim and renew community amidst a universe of competing groups and claims.

At the regional level, the Padma Saliyars assert their collective right to make ritual offerings, especially cloth as a fruit of the loom, during specific ceremonies at major temples in Tamil Nadu. At the level of the street, the group commemorates the original sacrifice of Bhavanarishi at the local shrine through a night vigil and invocation of the deity through the performance of communal ritual and retelling of stories and cosmic genealogies from the caste-purana. At the level of the household, individual transition rituals in the domain of work (daily and monthly calendar) and social status (life-cycle) reiterate observances of a sectarian identity. The avoidance of the loom during these occasions emerges as the articulation of weaving as a sacrificial offering.

In Major Regional Temples

Weavers among the lower ranking shudra castes have been known to have forged links with important vaishnava and shaiva temples in south India through their involvement in sectarian movements since medieval times.[23] Members of the Padma Saliyar community in the northern districts of Tamil Nadu remember their forefathers as *Lingavantaru* (carriers of the *lingam* or phallic emblem of Shiva) or *Virashaivaru* (staunch shaivites), while those in the southern districts of Thanjavur and Tiruchirapalli even today are initiated into the vaishnava sect by the *jiyar* (head priest) of the principal shrine of Vishnu at Srirangam. In Kanchipuram the *vellai chire* (white sari) and *manjal chire* (turmeric yellow sari) divisions correspond to the shaiva and vaishnava affiliations respectively. Affiliation to major temples have not only enabled the accumulation of rights and privileges by mobile and/or unstable groups but also facilitated their assimilation in wider society. In what follows, I examine the Padma Saliyars' participation in periodic festivals and ceremonies as spatialised claims of community within ongoing redistributive processes of regionally significant temples in Tamil Nadu.[24]

The Padma Saliyars say that the *Bhavanarishi Puranam* has conclusively established their right to present the flag cloth at all major Shiva temples in the southern territories. In Kanchipuram, the Padma Saliyar Sangam and local silk leaders have worked to successfully implement this mythically sanctioned privilege at the Ekambareshwara temple as well as at the temple of Shiva's consort, goddess Kamakshi, where I was witness to the community's participation at the annual flag hoisting festival with an offering of a 37-metre long flag-cloth woven at a cost of Rs. 50,000 (approximately USD 780).

In Kumbakonam local caste association officials referred to a dispute that occurred between members of their community and other weaving communities in the region, namely the Telugu-speaking Devangas and the Tamil Saliyars, over rights to ritual honours at the Uppiliappan temple of Vishnu in Thirunageswaram located in the outskirts of Kumbakonam. The Tamil Nadu Padma Saliyar Sangam are said to have succeeded in substantiating their prerogative at the temple by quoting their genealogical links to sage Markandeya whose image appears in the inner sanctum of this temple. Markandeya is seen here kneeling before the principal deities Uppiliappan and his consort Bhumidevi in a gesture that represents the act of officiating at a wedding ritual (see Fig. 4.4). That Markandeya is the father of Bhumidevi and Vishnu is his son-in-law is attested to even in the *sthala purana* of the temple and described as Myth 4 as part of the caste group's claims to a cosmic lineage

Fig. 4.4: An invitation to the eightieth birthday celebrations of K. G. Ramaswami Chettiar depicting the inner sanctum of the Uppiliappan temple at Thirunageswaram, Thanjavur district.

Source: Author's copy.

and affiliation to this particular vaishnava shrine. The Padma Saliyars argue that since goddess Lakshmi (as Bhudevi) is the daughter of their ancestor Markandeya, they too are members of her natal family, thereby making Vishnu, in the form of the presiding deity of the temple—Uppiliappan—their son-in-law.

The marriage ceremony (*thirukalayaanam*) between the Lord and his consort, Bhumidevi, is held annually in the month of Aippasi (October 15–November 15) on the day of the *thiruonam natchaththiram* (asterism)[25] regarded by vaishnavas as the star of Vishnu in his shrines at Tirupati (Andhra Pradesh) and Uppiliappan in Thanjavur (Tamil Nadu). In the annual cycle of the sun, the month of Aippasi falls in the 'dark' half of the year when the sun is travelling southward (*dakshinaaya*) in relation to the equator. This is the end of autumn and the beginning of winter when the *manes* (souls of the ancestors) are said to visit. On the darkest day of *amavaasaya* (no moon), *Dipaavali*, the festival of lights is celebrated to welcome their return throughout India.[26] It is also the period when caste Hindus are enjoined to ritually don new cloths. There is great demand for saris and weavers have just completed a period of intensive weaving. New garments or cloths freshly woven and removed from the loom, like the first harvest, are seen as first-fruits of labour. In order for them to be fit for human use they must first be offered as an oblation to the gods.

The wedding ceremony occurs after Dipaavali when weavers return to their looms after a period of *vratham* or vow of abstention from daily work activities. The apportioning of cloth (and other items of daily sustenance) as sacrificial offerings to deities marks their collective re-entry into the world of the mundane. The marriage proceedings are conducted before a sacrificial fire and jointly funded by the Padma Saliyars of Thirunagesvaram residing in the vicinity of the temple who are free to invite their kin from other villages to attend. As the family of the bride and as the original weavers of cloth for the gods, the Padma Saliyars exercise their right to offer items of gift (*siir varasai*) to the celestial couple which include unstitched garment-cloths, brass or steel vessels, flowers and fruits. The cloths are used to dress the images as well as offered in the form of oblations to the sacrificial fire, the desacralised leavings of which are returned to the sponsors at the end of the ceremony.

In the temple ritual described above, offering cloth to the gods is not merely an act of propitiation but constitutive of a regionally spatialised community identity through the agency of publically sanctioned rights and honours. The Padma Saliyars in Kumbakonam uphold their right (*mandakaappadi*) to make these offerings of cloth on the particular day as members of the bride's natal family and have defended it when the same has been contested by other weaving castes.

The next section describes the publically significant shaiva festival of repentance, *Mahashivaratri*, which also becomes an occasion to commemorate the original sacrifice of Bhavanarishi to reiterate and establish community at the street level.

In Street-level Shrines of Bhavanarishi

The historiography of artisan groups has emphasised their distinctiveness on the basis of their pattern of residence in segregated streets in and around temples. According to Ramaswamy, 'weavers were usually settled in the *tirumadaivilagam* of the temple .... In every town weavers had their own separate quarters. During the period of Uttama Chola (tenth century), the Pattusales were settled in the four quarters of Kanchipuram (called Kachchipedu in the inscription) known as Karuvulanpatti, Karisahanappatti, Atimanappatti and Eruvalichcheri' (Ramaswamy 1985a: 16). Arterburn's (1982) ethnographic evidence from Kanchipuram corroborates the historical concentration of weavers in virtually homogeneous streets which often crisscross with streets belonging to other castes in and around major temples.

Attending to spatial practices associated with smaller, lesser known community-specific shrines like that of Bhavanarishi, however, allow one to examine how a weaving group deploys ritual practices at the level of the street to articulate a shared and distinctive identity. The Padma Saliyars often refer to the shrine of their mythic ancestor as a *matham* and distinguish it from a *daivasthanam* or temple. A matham (*matha* in Sanskrit) is different from a temple in that 'both architecturally and ritually [it] is inevitably focused upon the tomb of the founding *svami*.'[27] There is no *gopuram* or pinnacle and the ritual service includes the singing of *bhajans* or devotional songs. According to Koppedrayer (1991), mathas together with their ritual symbols and complexes have been deployed by high non-brahmin castes to make public statements of their collective rights and privileges on the basis of a shared spiritual lineage.

Discussions with the general secretary of the Padma Saliyar Sangam in Chennai led to a list of Bhavanarishi shrines scattered across the state of Tamil Nadu. Mapping the location of these temples on a district-wise map of Tamil Nadu (see Fig. 4.5) yielded an estimation of the spread of the Padma Saliyars in the state.

Bhavanarishi shrines located in, or in the vicinity of, Padma Saliyar inhabited streets reinforce community through communal acts of worship, renovation and construction and are regularly featured in the monthly community magazine. Announcements of street-level festivals and sponsorships are made in the *Padma Saliyar Kural* through the agency of the district-level offices of the Tamil Nadu Padma Saliyar Sangam. The Bhavanarishi temple in Avaniyapuram in Madurai, whose scale and expansion in recent years marks the community's growing pre-eminence in the town, is especially significant in this regard. The renovation and extension of this shrine was undertaken by KGR for the benefit of the community and many important caste association meetings and functions are held here.

Worship in Bhavanarishi mathams involves the collective performance of rituals on the street level. Bhavanarishi is never venerated in the privacy of an individual's home. Life-cycle rituals like the *tali* or marriage locket tying ceremony are always conducted before female ancestors (*perantaalu*) and family deities like Angaaliamman and Periyaandavar, and not before Bhavanarishi. In fact, the image, photograph or any representation of Bhavanarishi is conspicuously absent from Padma Saliyar homes. As a *kulaguru* or community preceptor of the Padma Saliyars, Bhavanarishi's shrine is

Fig. 4.5: Map of Bhavanarishi shrines in Tamil Nadu [map 1: 2,500,000]. These shrines coincide with the incidence of Padma Saliyar concentrations in districts across the state. The map is based on a list of shrines created by the late S. Thilakendran, and updated by R. Venkatachalapathy, General Secretary of the Tamil Nadu Padma Saliyar Sangam, Chennai.

recognised as being distinct from other shrines of village deities (*naaduthevam*) and those of deities of extended kin (*pangaalithevam; vamshathevam; kulathevam*). Such shrines, often even makeshift, form the nucleus of exclusive community activity during important festivals for the benefit of Padma Saliyars in the neighbourhood.

Fig. 4.6: The Bhavanarishi matham on Singhaperumalkovil Street in Kanchipuram. Most mathams in Tamil Nadu have been renovated by local-level caste leaders by constructing a Dravida style temple tower and a ceremonial installation of the Bhavanarishi idol.

Source: Courtesy the photographer, Rags Raghavan.

The festival in honour of Bhavanarishi is usually celebrated in the month of *Thai* (January–February) soon after the Tamil harvest festival *Pongal*. It is observed by both shaiva and vaishnava Padma Saliyars in Tamil Nadu. In the mid-90s when J. Nathamuni was the caste headman and secretary of the local-level association in Swamimalai, the eastern subdivision of the Padma Saliyars offered worship at a shared matham on

West Raja Street, whereas the western subdivision performed the festival in their own shrine on North Street.

The *Bhavanarishi Puranam* provides the text for the hymns and chants sung during community festivals. The collective invocation during such times involves the ritual re-enactment of the life of their mythic ancestor and caste deity and is authoritative in prescriptive details for leading an ethical life. According to Nathamuni, 're-reading the purana during such occasions is good for the general prosperity and well-being of our community.'

It is imperative that all members of the community be available for the Bhavanarishi ceremonial, hence it is held during the period when weavers take a break from weaving after the heavy rush of sari orders for the Pongal season. Not only does the function herald the Tamil harvest, it also marks the end of the dark six months of the year and the beginning of the bright half (*Uttaraayana*) when the sun makes its journey into the northern skies.[28] The Bhavanarishi festival is of great importance for both the shaiva and vaishnava Padma Saliyars, and falls in the dark half of the month (*amavapatcham*). Otherwise considered highly inauspicious, this period is the time for penance and for self-offering in the form of bodily austerities. The ceremonies coincide with the ritual complex of Mahashivaratri (night of Shiva) when devotees worship Shiva as the *Mahayogin* or supreme ascetic.[29] It falls in the lunar month of *Thai* (January–February) or *Masi* (February–March) soon after Pongal harvest celebrations and represents 'a religious vow (*vrata*) or a duty (*niyama*), an obligatory rite ...' to be observed on the 'night of Shiva' that occurs on the day of the no moon of every lunar month.

During these ceremonies (which usually last three, five or seven days), the group must be in a state of *vratham* or vow of abstention until the sacred installation is removed. Not only do they abstain from food and sex, it is also obligatory (*kattupaadu*) to refrain from carrying out the everyday tasks of weaving. The injunction to abstain from working the loom is enforced by the subdivisional community head (nattanmaikaran) under whose authority a public announcement of the same is made at least three days in advance. Any violation of this rule is liable to penalty by him. Weavers recall that in the past 'we shuddered at having to pay a fine or having the treadles of our looms confiscated by the caste headman' on account of the injunction against *midhiadi* or pressing the feet imposed by the caste association.

An important feature of the sacred installation of the community deities of the Padma Saliyars is their circumambulation (*purappaadu*) in the streets belonging to the particular subdivision of the community. Bronze images or consecrated pots (*kumbham*) representing the deities Bhavanarishi and his consort Bhadravati are the objects of veneration. The two deities placed on their respective vehicles (*vahanas*) are carried in procession amidst loud chanting of songs (*strotras*).

The collective incantation recalls Bhavanarishi's original sacrifice of creating the loom from his own body-parts for the benefit of his descendants, the Padma Saliyars. Some members of the group together with the local *bhaagavathar/ bhadiyaalu* or specialists in community lore perform rituals of self-flagellation using the sword of the rishi amidst loud chanting, which reaches a crescendo as the procession returns to the shrine with the sacralised pots or images representing the deities. The second day of celebrations is the day of no moon (*amavasaya*) and commences with a nightly vigil when the group members, all in a state of strict *aachaaram* or ritual purity, stay awake through the night, singing devotional songs (*bhajans*), watching mythological performances and listening to the narration of episodes from the *Bhavanarishi Puranam.*

On the third and final day of the ritual period of collective sacrifice, a combined unction (*goshti abhishekam*) of the images of Bhavanarishi and his consort marks the end of the neighbourhood ceremonial, allowing the particular subdivision of the Padma Saliyars to return to normal life.[30]

Upon return to Swamimalai in 2015 with Kaliya Perumal, who has taken over the duties of caste headman after the demise of Nathamuni, I was told that even though only seven Padma Saliyar families continue to weave here, the role of the

Fig. 4.7: Bronze images of Bhavanarishi and his consort installed in the shrine at Tirucheri, the original home of Radha Silks, 1995.

Source: Author.

caste headman as a ritual and social functionary for the street-level caste grouping remains. 'Who will handle the giving and taking of wives for Padma Saliyar households? We are all migrants to this town and there is no one to handle temple duties for us. We have had to establish our presence here by building and renovating temples wherever our community members reside.' The *mariyaathai* or honour of the group must continue to be represented at religious festivals in local and regional temples of Shiva and Vishnu.

At the Level of the Household

Rituals of sacrifice, involving a sacralisation and de-sacralisation, affirm the Padma Saliyars' collective identity with the cosmos at regional and street-level temples and shrines. A separate and distinctive caste identity is reiterated even at the level of the household where domestic rituals of transition serve to constitute weaving as a sacrificial offering. Here ritual attitudes and observances towards the loom mark transitions in the life of an individual. During these rites of passage the loom is hedged in with ceremonial acts which valorise weaving as a sacrificial activity. The location of the loom is always central in the living space occupied by the family. At certain fixed times the loom is made the object of ritual abstention. Weavers forego (*thyaagam*) weaving, regardless of the urgency of the task and the monetary gain to be accrued from it. They see themselves as being in a state of vratham or fast, which entails an offering of daily labour and forms part of a wider complex of beliefs that link body and cosmos in quotidian life.

The daily cycle of work in a weaving household is consciously aligned to cosmic time-space trajectories. Each day weaving commences only after having carefully consulted the ritual calendar (*panchaangam*) indicating periods of danger and harmful influences. A single day may be characterised as wholly or only partially auspicious or inauspicious depending upon these time periods. Certain planetary conjunctions (*yokas*) are considered auspicious and have the effect of enhancing the quality of the task begun at the time.[31] Weavers, therefore, prefer to ply the shuttle, lay the warp, remove a finished sari, or deliver it to the merchant, during time periods known as *siddhayokam* and *amritayokam*. The *maranaiyokam* is considered inauspicious and weaving and other related activities are generally proscribed during this period. Weavers say that 'the pit is the *yaaga kunda* (sacrificial fire) before which we perform our *japam* or incantation,' referring to the act of weaving as a sacrificial offering. Appropriately, an auspicious time must be ascertained before weavers enter the pit and before handling the shuttle carrying the weft and pressing the treadles in the ground below. Weaving commences only after an invocation recounting the original sacrifice of Bhavanarishi, from whose body the loom emerged in the first place.

The weaver's body is also a site for ritual abnegation. The periodic ritual of amavaasaya or no moon is observed among the Padma Saliyars in the form of a monthly vratham which the weaver undertakes both as the sacrificed and as the beneficiary. The new moon day, falling in the dark half (waning) period of every month is known as amavaasaya and considered to be the darkest day (*irrunda naal*) of the month. As already explained it is the period designated especially for the monthly worship of Shiva. It is also the day in the month when oblations are made to ancestors for the general welfare of the family. A cycle of oblations made during this period is believed to be equivalent to a year-long sacrifice.[32] On this day, members of the community must be in a state of voluntary abstention. It is the day when Padma Saliyars of both the east and west divisions in Swamimalai unite in the observance of individual ritual abstinence. They must eschew food and sex and, most importantly, refrain from weaving for the entire day. The proscription on operating the loom, specifically the treadles located in the pit below floor level, is a grave transgression equivalent to breaking one's fast and highly inauspicious.

Amavaasaya is considered to be a period of immense ambiguity but, at the same time, 'is said to be of the character of the day, of the sun .... While the new moon itself partakes of the character of darkness, it is also the harbinger of light and marks the beginning of the bright fortnight.'[33] In this respect it represents a re-entry or return and is indicative of the propitious commencement of weaving after a dark period of abnegation and austerity. On this day weavers rarely remain within the precincts of their homes, which are spaces of work and immense toil on normal days. In Swamimalai, the end of this period is marked by a collective ritual or *pujai* at the local vaishnava temple of Varadaraja Perumal, considered to be their *sontha* or own temple and patronised (and renovated) by members of their community (*samughathinar*). Unlike Bhavanarishi shrines, these temples are worshipped by other castes and are important in as much as they highlight the Padma Saliyars' affinal relation to lord Vishnu vis-à-vis other caste groups. Padma Saliyar families in Swamimalai maintain the exclusive privilege (*mandakappadi*) to perform a special ritual before the deity of this temple on every amavaasaya. The privilege is managed and regulated by the caste headman or nattanmaikaran who rotates the community's participation so that each and every household under his jurisdiction gets an opportunity to participate. Worship at this temple marks the end of a dark period of austerity and the beginning of a new weaving cycle in the auspicious period of the bright half of the lunar month.

Ritual pollution during individual rites of passage are also seen to influence the entire street of weaving households, particularly that of the subdivisional community head or nattanmaikaran, who joins the affected household in the ritual avoidance of the loom, albeit for a shorter period. At times of birth, marriage and death, not only the principal actors but other members of the household also abstain from weaving. During such occasions the weaving pit is temporarily covered and the loom and its accoutrements rolled up and kept aside until the ceremonies are over. The average period of birth and death pollution is usually three to five days, but the mother who has given birth and the principal mourner at a death continue to abstain from the loom for a much longer period. Weaving is resumed by all only after a purificatory bath and invocation to Bhavanarishi. Community is once again spatialised here through a sacralisation of the loom within the household to reiterate a shared, cosmically ordained work identity.

ENDNOTES

1. Ramaswamy 1985a, and 1985b; Stein 1980.
2. Ramaswamy 1985b: 420.
3. Das 1982: 14–15.
4. I have come across numerous Tamil and Telugu versions of the legend of sage Markandeya featuring the emergence of Bhavanarishi from the flames of Markandeya's *homakunda* (sacrificial pit or altar). In Tamil Nadu the Padma Saliyars use the legend of sage Markandeya as a spiritual guide and discourse on leading an ethical and disciplined life.
5. See Roy (1997) for the socio-economic history of the Saurashtras in Madurai.
6. Haynes and Roy (1999) have shown how expansive production arrangements in handloom weaving in south India during the colonial period attracted new entrants, many of whom were neither local or hereditary weavers.

7. Das 1982.

8. Bonazzolli 2003: 162.

9. The myths recounted here are translated from the *Bhavanarishi Puranam* translated from Sanskrit by Chettiar (1905). I am grateful to a number of people who helped me read it in Chennai: Sujatha Venkatesh and L. Kannan during our time at the PPST group, A. S. Krishnamurthy, Telugu and Tamil scribe/chronicler of the caste association and Kokila Ramakrishnan, my scholarly neighbour in Chennai.

10. The hank yarn wrapped around crossed knees in a seated position during the preparatory process of winding is a common sight in weaving households in south India.

11. These sons, with names such as Virashaivan, Vijayan, Viraraghavan, Vikraman, Chandraguptan, Bhanuvan, Jayan, Jayamartan, Chittan, Chitravirodan, Vastravidyavinodan, Mayamayan, Sarthuran, are all said to be equally intelligent, learned and brave as their father.

12. In Hindu mythology, *yuga* refers to the different eras of the world. *Krita yuga* is the first age through which the world must pass; *Treta yuga* is the second age of the world; *Dwapara yuga* the third; and *Kali yuga* is the fourth or present age which will endure for 4,32,000 years.

13. Cited in Thurston and Rangachari Vol. 5 [1909] 1987: 451–52.

14. Das 1964.

15. Ramanaiah, n.d.: 3.

16. Dallapiccola 2010: 226–31.

17. Appadurai 1974; Brimnes 1999.

18. Usually founded by vaishnavas from the 'touchable' shudra castes, these deviant orders attracted followers from among the trading and artisanal castes as well as those outside the caste system (Chatterjee 1989: 21–31).

19. Stein 1968; Tambiah 1982; Bradford 1985.

20. Thapar 1982: 296–7.

21. Reiniche 1987: 96–9.

22. Hubert and Mauss [1964] 1981: 13.

23. Stein 1968, 1977; Appadurai 1974, 1981; Mines 1984; Bradford 1985; Ramaswamy 1985a.

24. The redistributive process in south Indian temples involves moral and economic transactions organised through gift deeds and endowments that guarantee the conferral of honours and privileges to specific donors who have accumulated such rights over time (Appadurai and Breckenridge 1976).

25. The Tamil calendar recognises twenty-seven asterisms or stars along the monthly lunar cycle. The moon traverses one or more asterism daily. Each is believed to be associated with a particular deity or mythical event, which is then commemorated each time the day of the asterism returns (Clothey 1982; Merrey 1982).

26. cf. Clothey 1982; Merrey 1982.

27. Bradford 1985: 81.

28. Clothey 1982: 175.

29. Long 1982: 190–4.

30. Thurston describes the festival of Bhavanarishi among the Padma Sale in his volume on the castes and tribes of south India: 'A festival in honor of this deity is celebrated annually, during which the god and goddess are represented by two decorated pots placed on a model of a tiger (*vyagra vahanam*), to which, on the last day of the ceremonial, large quantities of rice and vegetables are offered, which are distributed among the loom-owners, pujari, headman, fasting celebrants, etc.' (Thurston and Rangachari [1909] 1987 Vol. 5: 449).

31. cf. Clothey 1982: 178.

32. Merrey 1982: 12.

33. Ibid: 16.

FIVE

REPRODUCTIVE HOUSEHOLD
Work, Loom and the Body

Myths and rituals enunciate weaving as a shared identity not only at different spatial levels of religious participation but also infuse the loom space and the regular activities around it in the household. The fact that weaving is more than a practical pursuit in the Padma Saliyar world view is apparent from the ritual proscriptions imposed on the loom at different times in the weaving cycle and its association with conceptions of body, space and cosmos. The conscious articulation of the loom as more than a socio-technical instrument of work, however, emerged quite by chance, and rather obliquely, over a question posed to Nathamuni, the community sub-divisional head, with regard to the making of the bronze image of Bhavanarishi installed at the matham under his charge.

Swamimalai is known for its bronze casting tradition and images for worship in temples and individual homes are produced here by *sthapathis*, a sub-group of the Viswakarma community of sculptors in the region. Nathamuni decided to introduce me to S. Devasthanapathi Sthapathi, whose grandfather had cast the bronze idol in question. The procedure for commissioning an idol, they explained, involved a careful reading of the *panchangam*, the lunar calendar and guide used by both bronze casters and weavers, not only for marking festivals and dates for significant rituals but also, and importantly, as a daily reckoner for identifying an auspicious time to commence a new work project. If I were to commission a bronze idol for instance, the sthapathi will need my birth star (or stellar constellation at the time of birth) in order to correlate my bodily presence or physical being to an existing temple in Tamil Nadu by matching my star with that of its presiding deity. Aligning an individual's astrological coordinates with those of the deities of temples in the region emerged as a process of cognitive re-orientation within a cosmic geography in accordance with which both Nathamuni and Devasthanapathi practice their individual vocations.

In the exploration of caste and subaltern consciousness, Chatterjee calls for the recovery of 'common sense' as a methodological lens and to make 'critical an activity which already exists in popular life.' I consider the rhythm of activities around the loom as 'common sense' pertaining to a commonly held set of beliefs and activities around work, rather than as an aspect of caste, class or craft superimposed from above.[1] Probing into the co-relations between work processes, the loom and the body in the daily life of the weaving household has the potential to bring out contradictions underlying the conscious articulation of a sectarian identity among the Padma Saliyars. The self-evident or obvious character of a practical activity is dispelled precisely at the moment when multiple versions of common sense collide to expose 'the conceptual realization of hegemony.'[2] This is the only profession where codes of conduct appropriate between unequals are flouted according to Nathamuni: 'We remain seated at our looms even in the presence of a superior as weaving must continue uninterrupted for the sustenance of the household. Such is the nature of our work.' In what follows I inquire into the popular and the particular of weaving practice to draw out the implicit and explicit aspects of the Padma Saliyars' claim to the right to weave as a cosmic bequest in the wider social order.

In a classic study of the loom among Tukolor weavers of Senegal, Roy Dilley (1987) has explored weavers' conceptions of the loom as embodying a mythic weaving ideology. The loom is viewed not only as a personal space constructed in accordance to an individual weaver's bodily proportions but also a ritual space for worship revealing a shared conception of weaving as an act of prayer. Weavers' resistance to modifications of the basic technology and structure of the loom, according to Dilley, is comprehensible only if one attends to the context of meaning within which the instrument of work/worship is embedded in the Tukolor world view.[3] Similarly, Messick (1987) demonstrates how the 'nonpublic, silent quality' of the historically specific discourse of subordination among women weavers in North Africa can be teased out by examining the loom as a site of a distinct female-centric weaving ideology countering the dominant gender discourse. Padma Saliyar conceptions of the loom as a body (of their mythic ancestor) gesture toward the entanglement of the metaphysical with the material in the daily quest for sustenance through weaving. Reconsidering the common sense underpinning a weaving household as an arena for the functional division of labour, in what follows I explore Padma Saliyar conceptions of weaving as a commensal activity, and the household as a locus of everyday consumption and nourishment.

ARENA OF COMMENSALITY

Nurturance or care and attention of the body, both human and nonhuman, i.e. the loom conceived as the body of Bhavanarishi, is a shared belief pertaining to activities related to the making of food and cloth. 'Attending to the loom is like tending to the dietary requirements of the body' explains Nathamuni. Cooking and weaving are metaphors for the general sustenance and reproduction of the household unit or *kudumbam* and alludes to both the physical unit and the familial unit. The living, consuming body of a member of the household is juxtaposed with the body of the loom as it consumes yarn for nutrition. The weft yarn (*udai*), strictly speaking, is not part of the permanent loom apparatus. It is perceived as *aahaaram* or food which is 'fed' into the loom. And just as food requires an unsoiled atmosphere and space conducive to cooking, yarn must be made pliable for weaving. It must be moistened (the weft pirns are always kept dipped in a bowl of water) and the woven end of the warp brushed with a gum and/or oil solution, thereby imparting the warp threads with a certain elasticity and tensile strength to withstand the varying degrees of tension on the loom and the friction from constant beating-in of the weft. It is necessary therefore for the loom to be located indoors and under focused lighting in an overall shaded interior of ambient temperature.

Anthropologists have examined conceptions of weaving cloth among different communities to demonstrate the ideological privileging of the loom as an instrument of sustenance and reproduction. Among the Kabyle of Algeria, Bourdieu (1977) notes that weaving is analogous to both ploughing and procreation and that cloth is a product of birth. A connection between birthing and weaving has also been made in the case of the 'back-strap' or 'loin-loom' of the north-eastern states in India by Iyer (1967) and by Apffel-Marglin (1993) in the context of cotton weavers in Orissa. Its particular form (a strap wrapped around the hip) and mode of bearing (the woven cloth emerges, as it were, from the loins) during the weaving process is metaphorically linked to child-birth. That the weaving process pertains to reproduction is evident from the common saying among weavers—*Thai pola pillai Nulai pola selai*; just as a mother brings up a child, so also yarn fosters a sari.

Inquiring into ways of thinking about the loom (and not just the shared codes of conduct around it) with Nathamuni over days of reflection revealed commensality or eating, rather than birthing or procreation as the privileged motif of comparison. It was made clear that cloth must be woven just as food must be cooked for the general sustenance of the household. The regular insertion of the shuttle into the horizontally laid out set of yarns is the act of feeding the warp (for cloth to be woven) and the weft yarn contained in the shuttle is the 'food' interlacing the warp each time it is 'opened' by the action of the foot pedals or treadles. It is no wonder that at times of individual and collective abstinence it is this particular task that is the subject of ritual avoidance. And regardless of whether weaving is likened to eating or birthing, the loom is unequivocally at the centre of all vital activities in a weaving household.

SPACE OF LIVING/LEARNING AND TRANSMISSION

A weaver's house is typically roof-tiled, with an outer verandah and characteristic raised platform or *thinnai* leading into an inner courtyard. The atmosphere of light and shade within the household permits the rhythmic work of winding, warping and weaving even as the verandah offers participation in the social life of the street outside. The distinctive street-wise arrangement of these houses allows individual households to always be in a position to garner support in the preparation of the yarn from their neighbours on the street. At such times the shady lengthwise space of the street becomes an extended space of work and mutual cooperation.

The looms occupy the longest room in the house, the *kuudam thaavaram*, or hall adjacent to the open courtyard. Unlike the Muslim Ansari weaving household in north India where the looms are kept outside the main living area in a shed known as the *mardaana* or male work sphere, in Tamil Nadu the loom, much like the cooking oven, is a permanent feature and constitutes the core of the overall plan and architecture of the house. Its installation requires the excavation of a pit below the floor level over which is fixed a frame comprising pillars supported on one side by a wall and on another by the roof. In the event that the rafters of the house are not at a suitable height from the ground, a wooden frame, supported by the nearest walls, is constructed above the loom apparatus to serve the same purpose. Once positioned, this frame becomes part of the structure of the house and is not easily dismantled without damaging its foundations. A change in the number of adult members in a household on account of death or marriage is reflected in the structural alteration of loom pits and the skylight directly above it.

As in the case of house building, loom installation also requires the invocation of *vaastu purusha*, the mythical being said to reside in the ground. The worship (*vaastu pujai*) involves adherence to certain prescriptions prior to unsettling the earth for constructing the loom pit. Weavers believe that if this ritual is either omitted or not performed rigorously then the loom will not prove to be beneficial to the weaver. It is dug in accordance to correct procedures (*nalla murraigal*) of loom installation that involve a matching of the planetary positions of the weaving cycle with that of the individual's horoscope or planetary positions at birth. It must therefore never be destroyed randomly but left covered if not in use or ceremonially re-installed for a different weaver.

Most of the Padma Saliyar weavers' homes I visited had more than one loom; the number of *kuzhi taris* or pit looms in a weaving household usually indicates the number of practicing adults at the time of constructing the house. Extra looms after the house has been built are added using raised platforms on the opposite end of the existing pit loom and the warp stretched above the latter's warp in order to conserve space. *Maedai-taris* or raised platform looms involve the construction of a brick podium against a wall to support the weaver in a semi-seated position above the floor level floor rather than inside the pit. Such looms are preferred by weavers residing in rented accommodation or in times of expansion when additional looms are required in the existing space, as they do not require major alterations to the house floor and wall structure. The warps of both looms are stretched lengthwise so that the warp of the pit loom is lower and closer to the floor while that of the raised loom extends above it. Weavers say that this arrangement allows them to continue weaving without having to interrupt their rhythmic movements on the loom to unwind the warp and re-adjust its tension.

In the mid-90s, with the rise in demand for silk saris from Tamil Nadu, some wholesale merchants had set up factory-

Fig. 5.1: A silk weaver's home in Kanchipuram where all members contribute to the household income regardless of age and gender.

Source: Author.

like production sheds, bringing together a number of loom workers from agricultural communities to weave under the same roof. Padma Saliyar weavers are rarely found in such situations. In dire circumstances they are known to leave the profession altogether rather than work in weaving factories outside their own homes. 'We are so used to working on our own time and in the comfort of our own homes that we are unable to succeed in any other profession.' Those who have left Swamimalai to work in hotels as security guards or in supermarkets work long hours and have to live in confined spaces and seek avenues to return. Others have set up their own shops selling tea or cloth (*tea kadai* or *javuli kadai*).

According to a saying among weavers, 'once you are able to weave a sari within twenty days, you are fit to set up your own household.' Equally, it is admitted that if a weaver wants to complete a sari in twenty days, he must get himself a wife. Families prefer to marry their sons to girls who are adept at weaving and capable of taking on the responsibility of the work involved independently. For the Padma Saliyars, weaving on the loom suggests a certain degree of responsibility appropriate to an individual's preparedness and level of skill. All the various stages in weaving—from preparing the yarn, to laying the warp on the loom, to the actual weaving of both simple and complex designs—must, in principle, be learnt by *all* members of the household regardless of their age and gender. In the Ansari household by contrast, only male children above six years of age are formally initiated into weaving. As adults too it is only the men who are engaged in weaving while women's work is primarily that of quilt-making.[4] Viewed as a joint activity sustaining the entire household, an individual can contribute to the different processes without his or her labour being marked as either specialised or subsidiary. According to this perception of work and labour, the household, or the domestic group comprising the young, old, and equally both men and women, is the productive and reproductive unit.

The various work processes are fragmented not according to exigencies of production time but follow the natural rhythms of the household and its members. In weaving there is no such thing as retirement. Cloth continues to be woven as long as its members are able to function without bodily impairment. Even in such cases there are weaving related tasks such as marketing and finance that require attention. There is no specialisation on the part of male weavers and women can perform all activities, from preparing the yarn to its actual weaving on the loom. This is made clear in the event of the death of one of the principal adult members, male or female, responsible for the domestic group. The male adult can equally take over the hearth and the female the loom, in case of such exigencies. All tasks that sustain and reproduce the household are viewed as important tasks. Younger members take over from adults as they gain proficiency and allow the latter to take on other tasks. Weavers proudly acknowledge that in their profession 'even the old have work to do.' Indeed, in a weaving household, weaving on the loom, like cooking at the hearth, must continue for the maintenance of the whole group.

The entire weaving process is learnt by watching and imitating those who are skilled in the task over a period of time. Unlike production under factory conditions, women and children are not sought for their 'unskilled' labour, but as apprentices who will eventually become adept in handling the various pre-loom and loom-based activities independently. The learning process involves 'catching the implicit knowing' of the different tools and techniques of weaving a length of cloth through the senses and repetitive actions of the body.[5] It coincides with the physical growth of the child and takes place in a context of observation and repeated trial and error. 'Just as a small fish learns how to swim, our children learn how to weave.' Initiation begins with bodily practice, of grasping simpler techniques through imitation, by assisting parents and other adults in the weaving household. For instance, children learn to recognise and sort rough or damaged threads and to repair them by twisting the broken ends with their fingers and binding them together with saliva. Embodied learning in the household confounds the naturalness of bodily 'skill' and reinstates learning as a social process rather than an abstract transmission of knowledge through textual or verbal instruction.[6]

Children become informal learners from the age of five years. They are allowed to watch by being made to sit close to the loom and get a 'feel' of the movement of the shuttle that holds the weft yarn. They are usually seen playing or sleeping in the vicinity of the loom and are accustomed to the rhythmic clacking sound of the cloth beater. By ten years of age they are well habituated to the movement and control of the hand-thrown shuttle. They have learnt to insert the shuttle into the warp (*naada podarathu*) but require an adult to press the treadles in the pit below. Children at this stage are also allowed to handle the minute strands of thread by winding the yarn from a bamboo horse onto the *parivattam* (also known as the *thiruvattam*) or spindle for preparing the tiny, finger-length, weft pirns for placement in the shuttle (*taar sutharathu*).

From fifteen years onwards, the height, arm span and bodily capacity of the trainees is adequately developed to handle the various parts of the loom and its processes. Their legs are now ready to reach and press the treadles for the opening of the warp (*paavu meedikai*). Their arms are also long enough to independently wind the weft yarn from the spindle and to enable steady movement of the shuttle, from end to end, across the width of the loom. The eyes and hands are also sufficiently sensitised to locate and repair broken threads and to draw in and twist the new warp onto the old (*pinnaithal*). The overall bodily alignment and coordination on the loom is honed now for controlling the simultaneous opening of the warp with the feet and the throwing of the shuttle with their hands.

By the time trainees reach eighteen years of age, they are able to weave without supervision and are well versed with the loom apparatus, the setting up of the new warp, assessment of the yarn and its appropriate handling for defect-free weaving, removal of a finished warp and folding of the sari and all other aspects related to the loom (*tari pati murraigal*). It is at this stage that an apprentice's mental and physical capacities are employed to full potential. Trainees are now able to judge the correct alignment of the warp and maintain even tension on the loom throughout the weaving process and become adept in the selective opening of the warp by pulling the right cord for producing the intended surface motifs. By now they are fully aware that weaving requires resolute discipline of the body and that an individual's practice marks the weave (*raham*) or construction of the woven fabric. The loom pit is usually granted at this stage and its construction is in accordance with the body proportions of the weaver in question. The other parts of the loom are erected in accordance to the dimensions specified by the pit.[7]

WEAVING: ALIGNMENT OF BODY IN SPACE

Most handlooms, unlike automated weaving technologies, correspond in scale and manipulation to the weaver's body. In the back-strap loom the warp is attached to the waist of the weaver, who is able to control its tension through subtle adjustments of posture. Similarly, in the pit loom the warp is placed just a few inches above the ground, in line with the weaver's navel who is seated below floor level in a pit dug in the ground. The measurement of the loom is in terms of *mozhms*, a unit of length determined by the distance from the elbow to the tip of the longest finger in an outstretched hand. It does not indicate absolute length, and is relative to the body of the measurer. The handloom's scale is devised in recognition of the organic limits of the body of the weaver who manipulates it, and not to the constraints of a standardised machine design. If two looms are to be installed, one for a tall weaver and the other for a short one, then the actual dimensions of each will vary without affecting the overall mechanism.

The loom's installation is based on a given proportion between parts whose reference point is the central axis of the loom in equilibrium with the centre of gravity.[8] On the horizontal plane, the loom's axis extends from the middle of the cloth beam via the comb-like reed and suspended lifting mechanism or healds (or heddles), to the floor peg where the warp is secured on the opposite end at a distance that varies according to the space available. On the vertical plane the axis ascends from the treadles, via the healds, to the pulleys that control the movement of the cord from which the healds, through which individual warp yarns are threaded, are suspended. The loom frame and the warp are always installed in accordance with these axes and are together balanced with respect to the centre of gravity. Weavers frequently employ the plumb line (*rasa kayir*) and/or spirit level (*rasa mattam*), both for the accurate installation of the loom and for ensuring that the warp is balanced.

Weavers manipulate the warp by aligning their bodies with the different loom parts along five focal points—the navel, feet, arms sideways, arms forward and back, and eyes and ears—during the course of weaving. This correlation is apparent from the way both the pit loom and the raised pit loom are installed. In either case, whether the warp is a few inches above the ground or raised above it, the peg securing the warp on one end and the median of the cloth beam on the other must always be in line with, or just below, the weaver's navel. This ensures the correct wrapping of the sari on to the beam as it gets woven. The centre of the sari width will then fall precisely on that of the cloth beam at every fold. The tension of the warp from the peg on the ground to the cloth beam (which alters as weaving advances) must always be balanced along the point identified by the weaver's navel, lest the warp becomes loose from one end and tight from another. The treadles in the pit below must also be installed so that the distance between them and the walls of the pit is adequate to prevent the weaver's legs from rubbing against the edges of the pit. Even their shape, width and spacing must match those of the weaver's feet (i.e. left treadle to left foot and right treadle to right foot) for even pressure to be exerted on them. The placement of the treadles inside the pit must, crucially, ensure their correct alignment with the heald pulley (optimal vision or eye span) on the one hand and, on the other, with the midpoint of the cloth beam which corresponds to the weaver's navel.

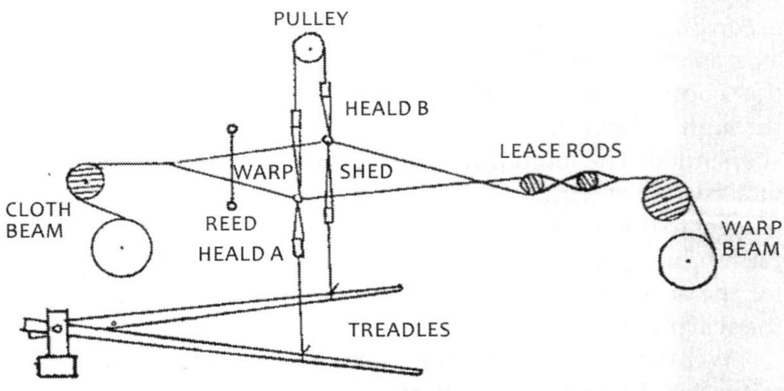

Fig. 5.2a: A schematic cross-section of handloom weaving showing the horizontal and vertical axes of alignment between the weaver's upper body close to the cloth beam, and the vertical loom parts manipulated using the treadles below.

Source: Adapted and redrawn from N. N. Banerjee 1977.

Weaving involves the continuous interlacing of the weft (a single thread wound on finger-length bamboo reels) at right angles to the warp (the set of threads placed longitudinally along the length of the loom). For the weft to be inserted into the warp, the warp needs to be 'opened.' This is made possible by the introduction of a discernable third dimension in the warp through the mechanism of the healds, which divide the warp into two sets of parallel threads and are attached to the treadles through a pulley. Each set of healds houses every alternate warp thread, which is passed through an 'eye' before entering the bamboo reed.[9] Pressing the treadles alternately with each foot causes the two sets of warp threads to open, thereby forming a shed or passage. The reel or pirn fitted into the boat-shaped bamboo shuttle carries the weft through the warp shed and must be beaten in with the cloth beater at every pick or each time the weft is inserted into the warp for the cloth to grow and develop a tactile thickness.

Fig. 5.2b: Weavers control the sari warp by positioning their bodies in such a way that the peg securing the warp on the opposite end and the median of the cloth beam on the other are in line with, or just below, the weaver's navel.

Source: Author.

The bodily movements required in the weaving process substantiate the correlation between the weaver's body and the different parts of the loom. The total width of the cloth beam does not exceed the distance between outstretched arms from side to side. The distance between the cloth beam and the cloth beater is no more than a single arm comfortably stretched forward to affect the to and fro motion of the beater. And finally, the pulley that loops and controls the cord suspending the healds from overhead must always be in the line of vision of the seated or semi-erect weaver. As the feet press the treadles to open the warp shed to permit the passage of the weft, the shuttle carrying the weft is inserted by one hand across the width of the warp. The cloth beater attached to the loom frame, and an arm's length away from the weaver, is brought forward by the other hand to beat in the weft at each shedding cycle. The unwoven portion of the warp is then brought forward by rotating the cloth beam so as to wrap the cloth onto it, and the entire sequence of activity is repeated.

METONYMIC UNITY: WORK, LOOM AND THE BODY

The body in Hinduism is a recurrent motif in comprehending the basis for the origin of the social order. A Vedic hymn constitutes the act of creation (in the natural and social world) as the sacrifice of the body of *Purusha* or 'cosmic being' and the human body as a cognitive vehicle and metaphor for society. Here the sacred confounds the mundane, and vice versa, so that the body becomes the site for the juxtaposition of the material with the abstract, the instrumental with the expressive, the corporeal with the metaphysical.[10] The interconnectedness of the human and nonhuman world, the moral and the physical is evident in traditions of practice of architecture, sculpture, painting, music, dance and theatre that privilege the human body not only at the level of form but also in terms of its relation to the everyday life of its creator/practitioner.[11] A devotee's identification and metonymic unity with the cosmos is complete not simply by entering into the microcosmic temple but, crucially, through the tangible process of worship within it:

> The worshipper of the temple is also the Vedic counterpart of the sacrifice as his physical body is also transformed to the body of the cosmic man .... this process of ... purifying the physical body of man to a point where symbolically he achieves an aspect of cosmic man is central to the architectural design and function of the temple as a proportionately reduced image of the cosmos.[12]

In the Padma Saliyar world view, the loom's association with the body of Bhavanarishi is not only at the level of myth but also in weaving practice. Identifying the different parts of a throw-shuttle pit loom with those of an abstract body, Nathamuni clarifies that each operative loom part corresponds to a body part not only in name and meaning but also in function and operation. I was able to draw up a table of these correlations with his help and illustrate the same with a line drawing of a pit loom and its identified 'body-parts.'

The loom-body correlation is mirrored even in the enunciation of the different activities involved in the weaving process as consumption and nourishment. The weft (*aahaaram* or food) is ingested and digested by the warp or intestine of the loom-body. It is held by the many pirns or fingers, placed into the shuttle or tongue, and passed through the open warp shed or mouth. It is packed or 'ingested' by the cloth beater housing the reed (teeth), which is itself set in a wooden frame comprising the upper and lower jaws. The process of interlacing the warp with the weft in this manner continues until a certain amount of cloth is woven (assimilation/digestion).

The conceptual unity of the loom and the body in promoting human sustenance and reproduction persists even at the level of work practice. In its care, and equally its abnegation, the body in the Hindu tradition appears centrally in the ethic and performance of work and activity in the material world. In Ayurveda, for instance, a doctor's diagnosis (and prognosis) is based on a non-dualistic conception of the body as the '... intersection point where two different orders of things overlap, physical forces ... and moral values,

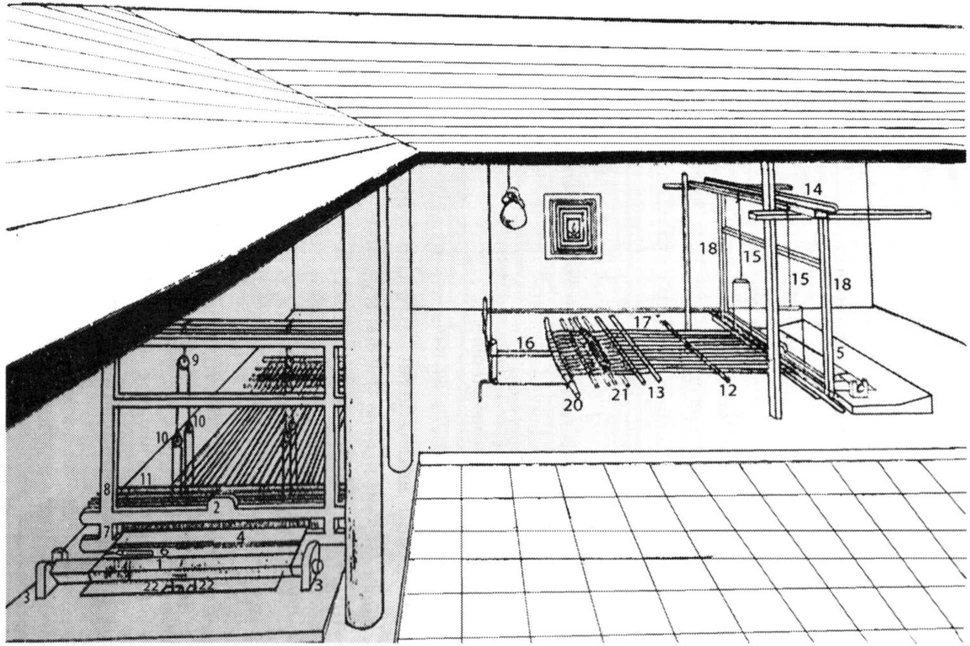

Fig. 5.3: An illustration of two pit looms in a weaver's home in Kanchipuram, 1997, with the different parts of the loom marked (see Table 5.1).

Source: Courtesy the architect, Arati Chari.

Table 5.1: Legend showing loom-body correlations

Number in Fig. 5.3	*Loom body part*	*Human body part*
A.	**Head and neck area**	
1.	Cloth beam (*padamaram*)	Head
2.	Cloth beater grip (*pidi*)	Crest
3.	Supports (*padamaram kaal*)	Ears
4.	Cloth width straining stick (*visaikarzhi*)	Nape
5.	Shed (*puni*)	Mouth
6.	Shuttle (*naada*)	Tongue
7.	Bamboo reed (*pannai*)	Teeth
8.	Cloth beater (*adikere palaghai*)	Jaws
9.	Large heald pulley wheel (*periya siir suzhattu*)	Eyes
10.	Small heald pulley wheel (*siriya siir suzhattu*)	Nostrils
B.	**Torso**	
11.	Healds (*acchu*)	Chest
12.	Warp support (*dandai kaal*)	Heart
13.	Flexible lease rods (*nesavu simbu*)	Ribs
14.	Overhead cross bar (*mel sattam*)	Spine
15.	Thin rope suspending hea ds	Nerves
16.	Loom coir/rope holding warp tension (*tari kayar*)	Principal nerve
17.	Warp (*paavu*)	Intestines
C.	**Upper Limbs**	
18.	Two vertical heald frame rods (*sattam*)	Arms
19.	Weft pirn/reel (*udai kutchi*)	Fingers
D.	**Lower Limbs**	
20.	Semi-circular rod holding warp beam (*udai kattai*)	Hip
21.	Warp beam (*paavusutha kol*)	Thigh
22.	Treadle supports	Legs
23.	Treadles (*midhi palaghai*)	Feet

Source: Author in conversation with J. Nathamuni, Swamimalai, 1995–96.

physical strength ... and the desired results of action.' Treatment in Ayurveda, therefore, consists of rules concurrently for diet (internal medicine) and action including bodily discipline, vocal training, and mental exercise.[13] Similarly, identifying and achieving oneness with the loom, both at rest and in motion, is at the heart of weaving as a disciplined practice. Body, technology and labour are united here through concentration (*chintanai*) and endurance (*porumai*), the two self-regulating chants (*japam*) by which weavers order their work life.

Weavers maintain that 'just as one has to expend one's saliva to eat one's food, so also one must exert one's mind and body to weave cloth.' Working the loom requires bodily restraint and control that must be practiced even by the most experienced of weavers. It is rare to find weavers who are overweight and lacking in agility. The interlacing of the warp and weft strands requires rhythmic coordination of the loom with the body of the weaver using focused and disciplined movements. A weaver's skill lies in transferring the pliability of loose threads onto the woven cloth. The introduction of the weft into the warp threads is made possible through two synchronous movements—the pressing of the treadles in the pit by the weaver's feet to create the shed and the simultaneous 'throwing' of the shuttle with his hands into it. For faultless weaving it is crucial that both these processes match. The warp must be 'ready' for the weft, which means that the open shed should not be skewed to ensure the smooth entry of the shuttle. Equally, the shuttle must not be thrown either too quickly or with too great a force, lest it damage the warp threads. The feet operating the treadles must also open the warp shed in perfect coordination with the right hand which simultaneously inserts the shuttle just as the left hand draws in the cloth beater to fix the weft into the woven cloth.

'A single glance outside the window, and you risk losing as many as eight weft strands' is a popular adage among handloom weavers whose undistracted attention is essential for cloth to be woven. Weavers position themselves in the pit in such a way that the back rests against the sloping platform on the wall behind even as the navel aligns with the midpoint of the warp and the cloth beam in front. All the mechanical operations of the loom follow in tandem with this posture for ensuring overall tension and balance in the weaving process. The feet are placed squarely on the treadles to affect the correct pressure on them. Pressing the treadles evenly will enable the healds to lift and fall equally. The torso is also braced to inspect the pulley above, whose unhindered rotation is crucial for the proper lifting and alternation of the warp even as the arms move sideways to pass the shuttle from end to end across the width of the cloth. The eyes and ears are continually attuned to the minutest change in the sound of the pirn spinning in the shuttle to instantly detect lost or broken threads.

For the Padma Saliyars, handloom weaving vindicates the genesis of an eating, breathing, growing 'cloth-body' whose structure is set not by the individual body of the wearer (body-cloth), but by the form of an abstract body with an internal coherence and autonomy of its own.[14]

The conceptual correlation of the sari with body principles was made apparent to me from the discussion on what was referred to as its 'carriage' or 'posture.' If the prescribed pattern of differential denting (insertion of number of threads in the teeth-like reed of the loom) in the different segments of the sari is not maintained, weavers say that the sari will become unbalanced. The analogy they used was that of a heavy torso/ body on very thin and weak legs.

For handloom weavers, the sari is not a stiff, solid piece of construction but a flowing body with a distinct corporeal identity. The tassels made from the unwoven threads in between two saris in a warp are the hair whose strands are cut and braided. The narrow and compactly woven selvedge protects the sari from wear and tear as do nails in a body. The borders on either side help maintain its balance and establish the laterality of the sari like hands and feet. Joined, yet separate from the limbs is the torso which is the middle segment of the sari. The distinctive face belonging to this conceptual cloth-body is the ornate end-piece while the embellishments in gold and variegated silk thread are like the flowers and jewels that adorn the face and limbs. The ground weave and texture of the sari is the cloth-body's surface skin with pores while the motifs and colours that alternate and repeat give the sari its mobility much like a body in motion.

Even the vocabulary of terms shared by weavers and wearers distinguishes the three essential parts of a sari as body parts of an autonomous entity. The end-piece is the *mundaani* where *mun* refers to that which is in 'front' in Tamil. It is also referred to as the *talaippu* which is literally the 'head' of a sari. The middle segment of the sari is called the *vodal* or 'body' of the sari. And finally, *karai* is the term given to the borders; it also means 'boundary' or 'river bank' and is aptly suggestive of the hands and feet dividing the body laterally. The word *pudavai* commonly used for the sari in Tamil Nadu also echoes an abstract body reference where *pudai* means 'bulge,' 'site' or 'location' and *vai* is 'to keep' or 'place,' gesturing towards placement, body contours and drape. Indeed the sari must be worn in accordance to the spatial orientation of its own body principles specified by the top and bottom, inside and outside, front and back. In the Tamil cultural idiom a sari without a border and end-piece ceases to be a sari and is considered to be plain yardage or *gaada* instead.[15]

ENDNOTES

1. According to Chatterjee, caste politics 'has drifted from one contentious principle to another (bourgeois equality, caste-class correlation, discriminatory privileges for low castes through state intervention, etc.) without finding adequate ground on which it can be superseded by a new universal form of community' (1989: 50).

2. Like Chatterjee, Herzfeld adopts the Gramscian view of common sense to reiterate anthropology's commitment to culturally specific forms of common sense and the often tacit complicity of individuals and social groups to their own subordination (Herzfeld 2015: 259–60).

3. Dilley 1987: 259–63.

4. 'At the age of 7 the male child ... comes of age as far as weaving is concerned when he stops sleeping in the *zanana*....' In contrast the female child 'is never formally taught how to weave.' With every year, until she is 15, she provides her services in quilt-making and is formally taught how to make them....' (Mehta 1992: 83).

5. See also Gamble 2001 and Marchand 2008 on embodied learning.

6. Lave and Wenger (1991) have discussed modes of knowledge transmission within 'communities of practice.' Herzfeld (2004) has used the notion of 'artifice' to discuss knowledge transmission as 'theft' among wood workers in Crete. For him apprenticeship, where knowledge is reluctantly passed on, is the ultimate expression of a potentially competitive relationship. Here apprentices do not learn from verbal instruction from their masters but are forced to 'steal with their eyes.'

7. See also Dilley (1987) for a similar account of how the Tukolor tribes' ideas about weaving play an important role in the way a loom is constructed and its dimensions determined.

8. The central axis (*kaya madhya sutra*) runs as an invisible thread of balance in the Indian sculptural tradition. In architecture, it is the smallest 'module' or cube represented as the *garbhagriha* or inner sanctum of a temple (cf. Ananth 1991).

9. The reed is a device through which individual warp threads are passed to keep them evenly spaced and horizontally aligned. A well-seasoned and cleaned bamboo reed maintains its own flexibility and keeps the warp pliant and prevents the miniscule silk threads from snapping easily.

10. Mauss 1973; Douglas 1970; Beck 1973, 1976; Das 1976, 1985.

11. Boas 1973; Vatsyayana 1983; Wayman 1982.

12. Vatsyayana 1983: 75.

13. Zimmerman 1979: 17–21.

14. Levi-Strauss has similarly described the significance of an 'object-body' correlation for the Caduveo Indians of the Northwest coast of America: 'the chests of Northwest Coast art are not merely containers embellished with a painted or carved animal, they are the animal itself keeping an active watch over the ceremonial ornaments which have been entrusted to its care. Structure modifies decoration, but decoration is the final cause of structure, which must adapt itself to the requirements of the former. The final product is a whole: utensil-ornament, object-animal, box-that-speaks ...' (Levi-Strauss 1963: 260–1).

15. '*Kai tari selai mundaani illamal, selaiye erkaadu. Adu selaiye illai*' [A handloom sari without an ornamental frontispiece is not a sari. It cannot be called a sari]. See Kawlra 2002 for an explanation on draped or unstitched garments as an aspect of Asian clothing cultures; and Kawlra 2005 for a discussion on the korvai technique, which involves the 'joining' of contrasting colours, as the technical articulation of metaphysical ideas on the conjunction of opposites.

SIX

MOBILISING VALUE
Authentic and Auspicious Design

Whether dead or alive, an elephant is worth a thousand gold coins. Kanchi silk too commands such a value, whatever its condition, old or new, tidy or damaged[1]

In the early 1990s the towns of Kanchipuram and Kumbakonam were famously associated with specific types of silk saris known as 'wedding' saris. Kanchipuram is known for its 'contrast-bordered' heavy silk and gold saris, and Kumbakonam for its lighter silk and gold saris characterised by their 'one-sided borders.' Place-based branding is also echoed in the retail display of silk saris at all major silk stores in the Panagal Park area of T. Nagar in Chennai, the principal extra-local market and commercial hub for the sale of silk handloom cloth from dispersed weaving towns and villages in the state. The specialised production of each weaving town in Tamil Nadu is popular knowledge and the subject of lively conversation among patrons who are quick to recognise and regale the features of an expensive Kanchipuram silk when compared with a Kumbakonam sari. These saris are valued not only for their characteristic weight, durability and lustre of the silk used but also for the bright contrasting colour combinations and purity of the silver plated gold wire used in the borders and end-pieces.

In the shared vocabulary of the weavers and their patrons, the three visually differentiated segments of a Kanchipuram sari—the edges or border(s), the middle or ground and the two end-pieces—constitute its design layout. Referring to the unchanged formal arrangement of elements in the contrast-bordered sari, weavers use the analogy of film: 'Kanchipuram saris are like films—the embellishments, like dialogues in movies, have been introduced only recently with the advent of devices like the dobby and jacquard.' Technical innovation does not alter this basic tripartite format of the contrast-bordered sari and instead is believed to further enhance its timeless appeal or 'traditional' value.

Artisanal textiles are visual texts that mediate and consolidate social relations through their 'capacity to communicate social identities and values' in a shifting landscape of social exchange, trade, geography and migration.[2] Exchange within a particular cultural and historical context, according to Appadurai, illuminates the 'commodity candidacy' of a 'thing,' (cloth in the present case) and 'refers to the standards and criteria (symbolic, classificatory and moral) that define [its] ... exchangeability.'[3] I focus here on the sari embedded within a matrix of exchange relations in order to render visible the practical and cognitive processes that unite, rather than distance, producers and consumers of the Kanchipuram sari within a framework of shared values.

Attending to the discourse of value surrounding the production and use of these saris in Tamil Nadu sheds light on the Padma Saliyar juxtaposition of the symbolic with the practical in authenticating their own relationship with the product of their work. Notions of identity and difference with an abstract body (loom-body and cloth-body) not only defend their genealogy as 'original' weavers but also guide their work practice and self-representation as producers of the 'original' or 'genuine' Kanchipuram sari in a universe of duplicates.[4]

ALIGNING WITH 'TRADITIONAL' DESIGNS

We have already seen how Rukminidevi's interventions in design and promotion of the Kalakshetra sari in the first half of the twentieth century led to an expansion of the appeal of the silk korvai sari as the dress of the 'classic' Indian woman. The changed profile of the elite as cinema actresses, singers, dancers and politicians post-independence, and the simultaneous rise of a new middle class across India in the decades that followed, further widened the demand for silk saris with a 'traditional' appeal. A survey conducted by Foundation to Aid Industrial Recovery (FAIR) in 1985 in the three major silk product markets—Bangalore, Madras and Delhi—revealed that 60 per cent of the demand was for 'traditional' silk saris whereas the market for light-weight modern printed, power-loom varieties was 40 per cent. The study also indicated a rise in demand for 'south silks' amongst the Indian upper and middle classes.[5]

According to the proprietors of both Nalli Silks and Radha Silks, the introduction of new designs was through a conscious revival of motifs, colours and patterns found in the sari collections of the brahmin and non-brahmin elite of Madras. Nalli's familiarity with them and their preferences is recorded in his book as follows:

> When I went to Kalakshetra once, I was able to see the arrangements there. Like Thirumathi Rukmini Arundale there are some other eminent women such as Thirumathi Prema Srinivasan of the TVS Group of Firms, Thirumathi Lakshmi Viswanathan who is famous in the dance field, Thirumathi Mrinalini Sarabhai of the Sarabhai group and Thirumathi Meena Muthiah who are giving their best attention to this field. They are rendering significant service to the silk industry by furnishing their own designs, and models of old designs so that they could be readily introduced and popularized. As a result a way has been found for us to get sarees and designs which were prevalent twenty five years back as well as designs

> which were in use about three generations ago. This is really a great blessing.[6]

Radha Silk Emporium in Mylapore had gone one step further when they hired Shanta Guhan, a prominent member of the Crafts Council of India in the 1990s, to offer advice on the design preferences of her circle of craft enthusiasts and to redo their store front window along the same lines.

Interventions in design were done at the level of state institutions where elite consumers of the Kanchipuram sari played a significant role in boosting the circulation of 'traditional' designs among silk sari producers and retailers in Chennai (then Madras). In the mid-1950s, the All India Handloom Board and the Tamil Nadu State Government established the Weavers Service Centre at Kanchipuram to provide new designs to handloom weavers along the design stipulations provided by Kalakshetra. Veerappan, a set designer at Kalakshetra, trained in sari designs by Rukminidevi, began using temple architecture and other 'tradition' invoking themes as inspiration for motifs in sari borders and frontispieces in what came to be known as a distinctly 'Kalakshetra' design and colour palette. The 1961 Census of India on weaving in Kanchipuram notes the mediating role of the Weavers Service Centre in familiarising cooperative societies and private producers with the 'traditional' tastes and sensibilities of elite consumers of the Kanchipuram sari:

> Experts frequently visit the weavers' cooperative societies and the dye houses of the weavers and give them the necessary advice .... The Ammapet, Coimbatore Devanga and the Koorainad Industrial Societies adopted some of the designs evolved in the Centre. In the private sector, Messrs. Petety Venkiah Chetty and Son of Kancheepuram and Messrs. Radha Silk Emporium, Madras, have taken advantage of the designs evolved by the Centre.[7]

By the late 1950s the silk weaving industry in Kanchipuram had witnessed a change in the varieties of saris being produced. The 1961 Census of India reports that despite fluctuations in price and availability of silk and zari yarns, a noticeable 'shift in design thanks to change in fashion set by the North

India women with their liking for silver lace' is discernable and 'more and more saris, especially in Kanchipuram Kamakshiamman Cooperative Society, are being produced with silver lace instead of gold lace and with increased exports to foreign countries and Delhi, Bombay and Calcutta ....'[8] A study conducted in the early 1980s suggests that the 'number of silk looms in the district increased by 67 per cent from 1961 to 1983, from 7,200 looms to 12,006.'[9] In 1982, when the Government of India imported silk yarn from China to meet this rising demand, silk looms in Kanchipuram were busy with fresh advances in sari motifs and textures.[10]

Similar growth was recorded for the neighbouring Arani and north Arcot region since the 1970s and 80s. What is noteworthy is that the expansion of silk handloom weaving during this period is associated with the rising demand for a particular variety of silk sari—one that employs the three-shuttle or korvai technique for solid-bordered weaving. Research findings by the Madras Institute of Development Studies in the early 1990s attested to a dramatic shift in Arani from simple varieties to more complex weaves along the lines of those woven at Kanchipuram.[11] Research conducted again in 2009 revealed that nearly three quarters of the weaving households in the Arani area were producing a sari variety which was considered to be a 'poor cousin' of the Kanchipuram sari.[12] This aspect was once again confirmed by Basile who found that,

> The quality of the *korvai* saris produced in Arani is not quite the same as that of the *korvai* saris produced in Kancheepuram, as the latter have more "grand" designs, and more *zari* and raw silk are used. Yet, they are currently marketed as *Kancheepuram* saris and have occupied a segment of the market that is intermediate between "low-quality" silk saris and the high quality genuine *Kancheepuram* saris....[13]

In both these accounts of growth, reference to an 'original' Kanchipuram sari gestures to the rhetoric of authenticity that has its origin in the colonial construction of the Kanchipuram contrast-bordered sari within a place-based typology of craft production. The growth of Kanchipuram as a prominent silk weaving town in the twentieth century is consistent with its elevation as a 'place of origin' of the silk korvai sari in official colonial and postcolonial records.

AUTHENTIC DESIGN, ORIGINAL PRODUCERS

The transformation of spaces of production into 'places of origin' occurred through a fictional mapping of artisanal production within a typology of craft under the British. Systemising local production realities in the language of craft, applicable throughout the length and breadth of the colonised territory, captured the geographical spread of the coverage in a single sweep and spatially marked craft products according to their ascribed 'place of origin.'

Artisanal products and processes were recorded in colonial texts according to rationalised classificatory schema with details of the raw material used, techniques employed, nature of ornamentation and provenance or chronology of ownership and location.[14] This process of entextualisation[15] of artisanal products within a place-based typology of craft in colonial documents not only linked specific products and processes to specific places but also fixed standards of quality to discrete localities within the idiom of the 'traditional.' The point is that the town of Kanchipuram emerged as a 'place' of production of the korvai silk sari through its entextualisation within a colonial cartography of 'traditional' craft.

The sacralisation of artisanal products as 'traditional' was accompanied by the perception of its producers as equally inhabiting the timeless space of an authentic past.[16] As part of the imperial agenda of territorial integration and administrative unity, producers were rendered static through the modality of caste-based census enumerations and other forms of 'sedentarization' of populations.[17] The invention of an overarching caste system, legitimised through other forms of colonial knowledge like historical epigraphy and ethnology, 'fixed' local communities within a cartographic paradigm of 'traditional craft.'[18] Artisans were accordingly emblematised in colonial records and exhibitions through rarefied conceptions of the 'native Indian craftsman' visually represented in the image of an anonymous ethnological 'body at work' in diverse exhibitionary complexes.[19]

The postcolonial appropriation of this colonial mapping of craft is evident in the numerous national projects that documented and mapped the 'traditional crafts' of India in census reports, exhibition and museum catalogues, craft documentations and maps as being uniquely associated with their geographical coordinates. The post-independence discourse of national heritage and development systematically inserted artisans within local histories, representing them as the 'living' repositories of an unchanged, even if fuzzy, cultural past. More recently, in the liberalisation era, artisans and their products are being drawn into a globally instituted legal branding instrument—the Geographical Indications of Goods or GI—that links a product's identity to a specified place and grants proprietary rights to 'original' producers within a wider national and international politics of place.

I began inquiries into the GI for the Kanchipuram sari in 2011, to find that the Tamil Nadu state's dispensation of the GI is predicated upon production compliance with the features of an 'original' Kanchipuram sari whose specific design and technical parameters are based on official colonial and postcolonial records that valorise a particular weaving caste—the Pattu Saliyars—as the original weavers of the silk korvai sari in Kanchipuram.[20] The GI refers to a time immemorial prior to the colonial period whose historical legitimacy is derived from British records that are clearly seen to be authoritative. According to the text, silk weaving in Kanchipuram is attributed to a caste of silk weavers, the Pattu Saliyars, who migrated from the lost maritime city of Kaveripoompattinam in the second century A.D. and served the royal needs of its many rulers down the ages, including the Pallavas and the Cholas.[21] This anecdotal account is an official statement of fact and its validating source is identified as the 1961 Census of India Report on silk weaving in Kanchipuram.

The text in the 1961 Census also sutures fictive and real accounts of local myth and history of Kanchipuram with the factual preponderance of the Saliyars in the town to establish an authentic explanation of the origin of silk weaving in Kanchipuram. It cites Sri Venkataswami Nattar's commentary (1937) on the Tamil epic poem, the *Silappadhikaram* as an authoritative source:

> ... the weavers mentioned in Silappadhikaram were really the Pattu Saliyars who wove excellent fabrics out of silk and cotton. When the maritime city of Kaveripoompattinam was submerged by the sea, it is quite probable that some of the Saliyars migrated to places of safety like Kanchipuram. This explanation is based on the fact that out of 6500 looms owned by different communities in Kanchipuram, the Saliyars own 1620 looms. Some of the original Pattu Saliyars of Kaveripoompattinam, which was submerged in the second century A.D., might have introduced silk weaving in Kanchipuram. As Kanchipuram was the capital of the Pallavas and came under the sway of the later Cholas, it is likely these weavers took to silk weaving to cater to the needs of the members of the royal family.[22]

The document goes on to deploy the colonial census classification of weaving castes to endorse the correlation between weaving skill, artisanal dominance and original producers of the Kanchipuram sari. The Census of India 1961 quotes from the Madras Census Report of 1891 the following: 'As weavers, the Saliyar were and still are more successful than the Kaikolans and Parayans. Subsequently, in the time of the Naiker Kings, the Saliyars were superseded by the still cleverer weavers of the Sourashtra country, the Pattunulkars.'[23]

The infusion of ethical valuations into work processes through the invocation of place is a marketing strategy among many artisan producers.[24] Retention of one's brand sovereignty is made possible through the active creation of an ethical divide between an 'authentic' and a 'fake' product through a complex narrativisation of local histories. The Padma Saliyars establish brand distinction and specialisation in a marketplace swamped with 'newcomers' or 'people who don't know what is weaving, what is texture, colour combination and design....'[25] It is not unusual therefore for new entrants into the silk handloom sari retail industry to invoke family biographies and rural roots, rather than work identities in their use of the past in value mobilisations. In 2006 Kanchipuram-based Padma Saliyar weaver-designer V. Sundarajan filed a formal objection to the Intellectual Property Rights (IPR) office in Chennai against the RMKV group (a relatively new silk sari firm from a non-weaving caste background) to contest their patent on a reversible Kanchipuram sari.

As a collective representation of the past, the GI for the Kanchipuram sari is an opportunity not only for the reconstitution of local history, tradition and place but also a defence of patrimony through proprietary rights on design and technique. Some Padma Saliyar silk producers and long-term residents of Kanchipuram see the state-led GI as an opportunity for a renewed branding of their products. Gaining legitimacy as producers of the 'original' Kanchipuram sari through the idiom of the GI entails involvement in its discourse of design.

Padma Saliyar Y. M. Narayanaswamy (YMN),[26] President of Silk and Zari Sari Manufacturer's Association in Kanchipuram and the first to have become an authorised user of the GI mark in 2006, says that the GI is useful in distinguishing the 'genuine' from the 'fake' Kanchipuram saris. He admits that customers must be made aware of the existence of this mark of quality. 'It is the difference between a horse and a donkey' and can prevent patrons of genuine Kanchipuram saris from getting 'deceived into purchasing imitations.' He has initiated a website in Tamil, Telugu, Kannada and English dedicated to this end which delineates the characteristic features of the GI marked Kanchipuram sari and is illustrative of the emergence of an authenticating rhetoric in branding and self-representation as the producers of the 'genuine' Kanchipuram sari:

> The main intention of our website is to describe the traits of Kanchipuram Handloom Silk and Jari Saree and distinguish it from fake silk sarees....**The queen of silk saree is Kanchipuram Silk Saree**. Kancheepuram silk

> and jari saree is being produced with the high quality twisted mulberry silk which dyed with palar river water, runs through Kancheepuram by the skilled and artistic weavers of Kancheepuram in handloom. The real gold and silver jari is used to produce the world famous kancheepuram silk and jari saree. We can know the worthines (*sic*) of The kancheepuram silk saree since it is registered under the **Geographical Indications Act**.[27]

According to YMN the instrumental and material value of the Kanchipuram sari accrues from the gold and silver content of the zari used, which he describes as an 'investment' equivalent to its value in gold. His brand rhetoric attributes a 'divine look' and symbolic/cultural value through its association with the town of Kanchipuram, well known as one among the seven holy abodes of the Gods and to the wearing of precious jewellery by goddess Lakshmi:

> When we exchange or sell our gold and silver ornaments we will get some value after deducting 30–35 percent of the value as wastage and making charge. In the same manner we will get such value of gold and silver according to the jari used in the pure Kancheepuram Silk and Jari saree after its maximum usage. Buying of pure Kancheepuram silk and jari saree is not an expense but it is also an investment. Wearing of pure kancheepuram silk saree produced with real gold and silver jari gives good things to our body and soul like wearing of gold and silver ornaments. It gives divine look like **Goddes (*sic*) Sri Mahalakshmi**.

The Kanchipuram sari is an archetypal product with a legendary nexus, not only with its 'place of origin' but also with its weavers who are seen as specialists in the accrual of auspiciousness (as distinct from the brahminical pursuit of the removal of inauspiciousness) for its wearers. The Padma Saliyars believe that adherence to specific design parameters in weaving the Kanchipuram sari and the ethical exchange of these saris will augment well-being and mitigate misfortune for the users of their products. Rather than an extrinsic state or condition characterising events and persons, auspiciousness for the Padma Saliyars is *woven into* the sari, mobilising value in the realm of shared work practice.[28]

SPECIALISTS IN *RAASI* OR AUSPICIOUSNESS

The Tamil term for auspiciousness is *raasi.* In its literal application, the word refers to a 'sign' of the zodiac to denote an individual's planetary constellation and is borrowed from Sanskrit to mean 'collection,' 'disposition,' 'harmony' and 'luck.'[29] Its usage is based upon the assumption common to South Asian systems of healing and astrology that humans are in a dynamic relationship with the socio-cosmic environment in which they exist. Achieving an appropriate state of balance with the universe involves a continuous orientation and re-orientation of the body in time and place. As time proceeds and as spatial directions change, humans also change their nature and condition as they are embedded in the very fact of continual change.[30] The use of a particular colour in south Indian ritual, especially in terms of its relation of association and contrast with other colours, according to Beck (1969) points to an alternation of states for ritual practitioners. Daniel (1984) uses the terms 'compatible,' 'appropriate,' 'equilibrium,' and 'conjunction' to describe the intersections of planets which, when seen together in their correlations, are harbingers of change.

According to this schema individuals, regardless of their caste status, are prone to both auspicious (*nalla raasi*) and inauspicious (*ketta raasi*) influences. For the Padma Saliyars, the intersection and conjunction of opposed elements and their transformations in the daily practice of work and life allude to the augmentation of auspiciousness as a desirable goal. Weavers are very particular about dates and time periods considered to be auspicious and meticulously consult the almanac often pasted or hung by the side of their loom before commencing the activity of weaving. We have already seen how the loom is installed in accordance with the weaver's own planetary configuration so that the pit is raasi or auspicious for the weaver. Work is the quest not only of material well-being, but also an accrual of 'good' influences in daily life. Given life's sorrows and joys, failures and fortunes, vices and virtues, auspicious procedures in weaving processes and in the exchange of the sari tend to keep the balance more towards the latter than the former states. Maintaining an optimal balance in the different levels—the pragmatic and the moral—in daily life, it is believed, will tend to shift the elusive bargain between the auspicious and the inauspicious in one's favour.

The relevance of this discourse in the realm of the practical activity of weaving for the Padma Saliyars is apparent in their pursuit of auspiciousness through an adherence to ethical prescriptions in the weaving and exchange of silk saris. Elsewhere I have demonstrated how the korvai sari is woven as a garment unit through the conjunction of opposed elements along three design parameters—colour and texture and ornamentation.[31] The korvai technique of using extra shuttles for border weaving highlights the 'design' of the sari as a draped garment by differentiating its three parts—border, body and pallav or end-piece—from each other and uniting them as an individual sari and separating it from other saris in the same warp. The value of these saris pertains not only to the price of gold and silver admixture used in it, but also to its non-monetary worth or raasi embodied in the way it is woven and sold or purchased.

Nalli Kuppuswami uses the language of metaphor to describe the protective (mitigating inauspiciousness) quality of the border-body-end-piece design format of the korvai sari to draw out its inalienable value beyond price for his customers. He shares his ideas in a semi-autobiographical ethical treatise titled *Work is Worship* (1983) written both in Tamil and English and distributed free of charge for patrons and members of his community: 'As the two banks of a river act as a check on the flood waters and prevent them from entering the village and causing damage and also help to canalize them to avoid wastage, the borders in a silk sari act as its fort to protect and preserve its beauty and color.' For him, the purity of gold employed is surpassed only by the ceremonial grandeur of its distinctive placement in the sari:

'Like the tilak (or vermillion mark of Hindus) adorning the forehead, zari adorns the silk sari.'[32] These descriptions of the design of the silk korvai sari exceed the aesthetic or functional and are explicit in their allusion to the wider context of use in augmenting auspiciousness for its wearer.

Silk and gold saris are principal objects of gift exchange at life-affirming ceremonies such as weddings, births, collective rituals and festivals in temples in Tamil Nadu. The wearing of and giving/receiving of silk cloths at auspicious occasions as well as offering them to deities in temples is ritually prescribed among many groups in south India. The sari of a married woman must be bordered, whereas that of a widow's is always plain and undifferentiated without any borders. It is this visual differentiation in sari design that marks a woman as a *sumangali*, literally woman with *mangalam* or 'auspiciousness' in south India and points to her ability to attract benevolent and life-affirming forces.[33] A wedding sari is distinguished by its colours—*arakku* (vermillion red) and *manjal* (turmeric yellow)—which are already part of a married woman's toilet. The vermillion red of the *pottu* worn on the forehead and the yellow of the turmeric used on the face and body are considered to enhance the propitiousness of a married woman. Writing about the colour combinations of the Kanchipuram sari favoured by the traditional elite in Madras, Prema Srinivasan notes that 'women favored the auspicious *pitaambaram* reds and yellows, either as separate colors, or in the same weave [i.e. in the same sari], or by marrying yellow and red warp/weft threads.'[34] Widowhood is marked by the divestiture of all these elements that augment auspiciousness in the daily life of a married woman.

In Tamil Nadu wedding saris in particular are never purchased at discount sales. Ideally, they are custom woven with the bride or potential wearer in mind. When this is not possible, saris are bought from reputable stores trusted for providing saris that are 'new,' and 'fresh from the weaver's loom.' It is not enough that a sari is woven in accordance to favourable alignments of persons and events in time and space; it must also be purchased at a fortunate time. In fact, the selection of a wedding sari and even the first stepping into a sari emporium after a marriage is finalised is done only after determining the auspicious day that will match with the individual horoscopes of the bride and groom. Women are known to buy the *muhuratham* or bridal sari only from the particular shop they believe to have proved to be raasi for their family.

Padma Saliyar owned sari stores in Chennai—Nalli Chinnaswami Chetti and Radha Silk Emporium—have acquired the reputation of being *raasiyaana* or auspicious for their respective clientele, who believe that buying the first sari soon after a marriage alliance is made from these stores will prove to be raasi for the newlyweds. 'Nallis is *raasi*' or 'Nallis brings good fortune' is a common phrase among families who are their long-term patrons. In fact Radha Silk Emporium in Mylapore is popularly referred to as 'Rasi' from the letters *Ra* and *Si* in their name but enunciates the word *raasi* to stand for auspicious. 'Women do not come to Mylapore to buy just any sari but the most important wedding sari at famous shops whose dazzling brocades are fit for a goddess or for a beautiful bride.'[35] So inextricable is the Padma Saliyars' identity with auspicious occasions that in the past a Padma Saliyar groom was made to weave his bride's wedding sari or the *kurai pudavai* which, apart from being a symbol of a fruitful marriage, constituted the auspicious act of marriage itself.

Padma Saliyars believe that to conduct one's life in accordance with certain 'good practices' (*nalla morraighal*) is simultaneously a heightening of the auspiciousness of the products of their work. Weavers of silk saris are known for their strict adherence to various prescriptions during the preparatory and weaving processes. It is believed that well-being will accrue if the *natchaththiram* (stellar constellations at the time of birth) and *lagna* (planetary conjunctions at the time of birth) of the weaver 'matches' that of the merchant's on the day weaving is begun. In fact the merchant's profit depends on this *vidhi* (practice). Even Lord Vishnu, the Padma Saliyars believe, is said to have given out the lotus stem yarn only after having selected an 'appropriate' time to commence weaving.

Failure to follow these prescriptions in the greed for more income may prove inauspicious and even harmful to the cloth, the weaver, the merchant, and even to the wearer of the cloth.

The sari, once taken off the loom, is susceptible to malevolent influences unless it is sold within a certain acceptable time period. The sari becomes 'old' even if it has not been actually used because it is said to have 'lost' its auspiciousness or ability to attract good fortune. Sari retailers seldom take back saris once sold because they believe that the sari is no longer fit for use at life-affirming occasions and ceremonies. Padma Saliyars are known for their ethical practices in sari retail and their customers trust them for not selling 'soiled' or 'used' saris that may have imbued unknown or harmful influences over a period of time. When customers insist on returning or exchanging saris they have purchased, the latter are kept aside for discount sales rather than returned to the shelves. In the Tamil month of *Aadi*, (mid-July to mid-August) otherwise an inauspicious period for marriages and other life-affirming ceremonies, Radha Silks holds their largest discount sale, known as the *aadi thallapadi.* Saris bought and sold during this period are done so with complete transparency. Both the buyers and the sellers are fully aware that the lowered price of the sari indicates the presence of a technical defect or design imperfection in the sari. Saris that have been on the shelf for longer than sixty to ninety days also, eventually, find their place in discount sales as they are considered of 'old' stock and not suitable as auspicious wear.

The Padma Saliyars believe that they are not just sellers of textiles but specialists in auspiciousness. This is apparent from the way they transact with their customers, especially those who come to purchase wedding saris. Once selected, the wedding sari and the groom's *veshti*, or bordered white lower silk garment, are ritually exchanged, not across the bill counter, but in the presence of the shop deity appropriately wrapped in a 'pure' white cloth with the auspicious vermillion and turmeric marks. Every day a piece of cloth, or blouse piece to be worn with a sari, is ritually presented to the last marriage party that enters Radha Silks. This is the 'Karpaghambal blouse-piece'

Fig. 6.1a and b: Purchasing a wedding sari is considered an auspicious act, as is entering this silk sari showroom in Kanchipuram (top). A busy day at the Sundari Silks showroom in Chennai (bottom).

Source: Courtesy the photographer, Rags Raghavan (6.1a); and Shankar, Sundari Silks, Chennai (6.1b).

offered daily to goddess Karpaghambal ('one who grants the wishes of all her devotees like the celestial tree, Karpagam') at her temple located in the vicinity of the showroom in Mylapore. Auspiciousness is so inextricably linked to the Padma Saliyars in Tamil Nadu that Nalli Kuppuswami is proud to claim that 'an auspicious time ... (can) be ascertained ... from the crowd found at the entrance to our emporium.'[36] Indeed, according to most almanacs, Tuesdays and Saturdays are considered inauspicious for making purchases and are also the days when silk sari sales are consistently sluggish.

Weavers say that it is the *thozhil dharma* or work ethic of the Padma Saliyars to adhere to appropriate procedures—from laying out the warp on the loom to the final weaving and selling of the cloth—to ensure the overall propitiousness of their work. The explicit moral correlation between the producer and the product in artisanal practice is also obvious in Sashikala Ananth's account of the theory and practice of the craft of the Vishvakarma group in south India: 'The sculptor learns to represent on stone, wood, metal, or earth the essence of his inner understanding ....The *shilpi* creates the *shilpa* out of himself as it were, and all his feelings are reflected in the manifested form.'[37] For the Padma Saliyars, to conduct one's life and work in accordance to ethical guidelines is to automatically heighten auspiciousness in daily life. These good practices of propitious alignments or conjunctions infuse their saris when worn or gifted and contribute to the balance in the share of well-being or misfortune, life-affirmation or its negation for individuals and groups.

The commingling of the symbolic with the material in the discourse of value encompassing the weaving and exchange of wedding saris in Tamil Nadu draws attention to the strain towards identity in embodied work practice. The accrual of raasi—a collective goal uniting producers with consumers—inhabits the efficacy of weaving and galvanises the exchange of the sari. Juxtaposing the metaphysical and the utilitarian in the rhetoric of authentic and auspicious sari design is a defense of shared cultural values in the pursuit of goals in daily life and challenges the axiom of self-interest in rational economic action.[38] It is also the way a group validates work as identity for itself and especially in dialogue and interaction with others.

ENDNOTES

1. Kuppuswami 1983: 39.
2. Schneider 1987: 415.
3. Appadurai 1986: 14.
4. See Kawlra 2014 for a detailed discussion on the production of 'duplicates' in Kanchipuram.
5. Sinha 1990: 40.
6. Kuppuswami 1983: 94–5.
7. Census of India 1961a: 35–6.
8. Census of India 1961b: 33.
9. Bharathan 1985: 94.
10. In 1982–83 the Central Silk Board estimated the overall domestic silk market to be Rs. 1,100–1,200 crores, of which the share of the silk sari alone was Rs. 1,000 crores (Sinha 1990: 40). Designs for 'Kanchina' saris using Chinese yarn as warp and Mysore silk for the weft were developed in large numbers by the Weavers Service Centre in Kanchipuram and Cooptex Design Centre in Madras (Bharathan 1985: 96).
11. Nagaraj et al. 1996.
12. Arivukkarasi and Nagaraj 2009: 41.
13. Basile 2013: 149.
14. Among the early projects of documentation that entextualised artisanal products for colonial interests is included the series of eighteen volumes produced by John Forbes Watson in 1866 and 1873, containing actual textile swatches and most importantly an appendix which spatially marked each example according to 'the places of manufacture or markets from which they came carefully enumerated under name, district, Presidency, or country, right down to latitude and longitude' (Driver and Ashmore 2010: 366).
15. I extend the notion of entextualisation from its original use in the context of spoken language in anthropology (Silverstein and Urban 1996) to that of enumeration of craft products. According to Raheja, entextualisation was the selective process of insertion of indigenous speech within colonial documents which 'radically stabilized and transformed their meanings and excluded or marginalized speech that was not congruent with colonial views of Indian society or colonial political interests' (Raheja 1996: 495).

16. The alterity of craft in colonial administrative discourse also denied coevalness to Indian artisans even if anthropology was the creator of 'allochronism' (Fabian 1983).

17. Irschick 1994; Stein and Subrahmanyam 1996; Washbrook 1997.

18. According to Dirks (1988), colonial interventions disassociated caste from its political context and local hierarchies, reconstituting it as an essentialised category and autonomous system of hierarchical ordering.

19. Dewan 2004; Mathur 2007.

20. See Kawlra 2014 for a detailed account on the institution of the GI for the Kanchipuram sari and how the GI's official standard of design, technique and place of manufacture is being subverted by a majority of the smaller producers and cooperative societies through the production of 'duplicates.'

21. Department of Handlooms 2005: 3.

22. Census of India 1961b:1–2.

23. Ibid: 2.

24. Fontefrancesco (2012); Paxson (2010) and Ulin (1996, 2002) have shown this for producers of jewellery, cheese and wine in Europe respectively.

25. This is the response from a Padma Saliyar Sangam office bearer from Kanchipuram upon being asked to comment on the proliferation of silk sari producers from other communities in Tamil Nadu.

26. Y. M. Narayanaswamy is well known in Kanchipuram as the protégé of K. S. Parthasarathi whose communist leanings in previous decades are at odds with his current market responsive stance.

27. http://kanchipattuzarisareeasso.com/English%20handloom/home2.html Retrieved March 2011.

28. The cultural value of auspiciousness has so far been examined as being distinct from Hindu notions of purity and pollution in ritual practice (see, for instance, Carman and Marglin 1985; and Madan 1991) and in ritual transactions pertaining to the universe of caste (Das 1982; Apffel-Marglin 1985; Raheja 1988).

29. Madras University 1982: 3423.

30. See for instance Obeyesekere 1976; Kemper 1978; Zimmerman 1979; and Egnor 1983.

31. Kawlra 2005.

32. Kuppuswami 1983: 35–6, 45.

33. The woman whose husband is still alive is considered to be a *sumangali*, but the devadasi who was ritually married to the deity was *nityasumangali* or one with 'everlasting auspiciousness' (Kersenboom-Story 1987).

34. Srinivasan 1983: 51.
35. Michell 1993: 120.
36. Kuppuswami 1983: 54.
37. Ananth 1991: 79.
38. 'Culture' according to Mary Douglas is not a discrete entity and involves the 'joint production of meaning.' The pursuit of auspiciousness is a dynamic process whose meaning emerges in social interaction and exchange in daily life and must be 'continually contested and always in process of mutual accommodation' (Douglas 2004: 88–89).

SEVEN

CONCLUDING REFLECTIONS

Silk handloom weavers and producers in India have been battling an economic and political churning since the beginning of the liberalisation era. Labour capital has been overridden by finance capital, shifting the balance in favour of the latter, buttressed by revenues from new businesses like tourism and real estate. Handloom weaving is fast becoming obsolete and weavers are migrating for jobs as semi-skilled or unskilled workers in catering, security, IT, automobile and mobile industries. Kumbakonam for instance, was a prosperous weaving town in the 1990s, but by the year 2015 its 'reserve army' has been spent. If farmers face debt and destitution through suicides, weavers face the same through desertion.

Returning to the field in early 2015, I found that of the 500 looms that once wove saris for KGR in 1994, only a fractional ten per cent remained. Most weavers had either left the profession or simply abandoned their homes without notice. Swamimalai, that once had 250 looms in East Raja Street and close to 100 looms in West Raja Street, is now left with just seven looms. These belong to ageing Padma Saliyar weavers who have remained on account of inherited property even as younger members of their household have migrated to bigger towns and cities in search of employment. The story of Kanchipuram is no different as it morphs from a centre of production into a retail hub of 'duplicate' Kanchipuram silk saris woven on power looms. Weavers who own their homes are abandoning the family profession as they pursue rental or retail revenue as a means of livelihood.

The contents of the community magazine suggest that upward social mobility through education is underway (see Fig. 7.1a). The *Padma Saliyar Kural* retains its readership as a marriage alliance bureau and receives contributions from Padma Saliyar silk producers and retailers in the form of silk sari advertisements. Ironically there are more prospective brides with educational degrees than grooms, a fact that draws

Fig. 7.1a: Cover of the *Padma Saliyar Kural* of January 2015, congratulating Padma Saliyar youth who have won state-level public recognition in higher education (Class X to undergraduate studies).

Source: Courtesy, Tamil Nadu Padma Saliyar Sangam, Chennai.

attention to the recent departure of handloom weaving as a viable and respectable livelihood option for young Padma Saliyar men.

Ritual privilege is also tenuous in the changing landscape at the turn of the twenty-first century. The spatialisation of individual and collective rights through temple honours occurs in a highly competitive field and anticipates disputes over territories of public acclaim. In Kumbakonam for instance, the new terrain for capital accumulation is marked by the economic pre-eminence of a Saurashtra 'big-man' and long-time neighbour and business rival of KGR. In 2015, the Uppiliappan temple in Swamimalai is no longer a site for Padma Saliyar articulation of rights to public honour. Instead, the prerogative has shifted to a Saurashtra leader and once reputed silk sari producer, Raya, whose recent acquisition of administrative control and renovations at the temple mirror the change.

We Who Wove captures a twentieth-century moment marking the growth and expansion of Padma Saliyar material, symbolic and political constituencies in the 1990s. The book signposts their prominent retail presence in Chennai during this decade; it points to the emergence of strong supra-local community-based production networks in the towns of Kanchipuram and Kumbakonam and villages in their hinterland; it notes the numerous philanthropic acts for collective advancement by Padma Saliyar leaders in diverse arenas from educational scholarships to temple/community hall construction and renovation; it records the self-conscious articulation of citizenship rights under the backward classes categories through petitions and articles in the caste newsletter; and it narrativises a shared aesthetic and ethic of work.

The Marxian insistence on a singular labour history has tended to isolate 'culture' from material activity, disassociating subjective ideas from objective conditions of production.[1] I have deployed an expanded notion of production, one that goes beyond the narrow generation of wealth and creation of discrete objects to 'the production of people and social relations.'[2] Social cleavages and subjectivities, according to this perspective, do not arise from a pre-existing or distinct sphere of meanings and symbols but 'are fully immanent in (produced by and productive of) this productive activity.'[3] The 'work' of community is also the mobilisation of value, continually pursued and created by productive action. Embodying the tension between those who are able to create, accumulate and sustain value and those who clamour to gain access to it, the enactment of community is a legitimate arena for investigation. In attending to Padma Saliyar safeguarding of caste-assigned artisanal rights, I have therefore taken the 'subaltern's view seriously.'[4]

The swelling of the ranks of unskilled labour, on the one hand, and clerical labour on the other, has been a function of the 'inconclusive debate' concerning 'technical education' and 'technical work' since the turn of the nineteenth century in India.[5] In the Madras Presidency this was exacerbated by the 'insulation of the artisan classes from any form of formal instruction in schools that could be classified as industrial or technical' and the emphasis on literacy as a prerequisite to Western-style education. Work and learning in a weaving household presents a sharp contrast to the alienation induced by technologies of production and surveillance in factories. It invites further inquiries into the modern separation between the manual and the mental in formal education.

The juxtaposition of the ethical with the aesthetic and the instrumental in weaving praxis has meant the reclamation of body discipline and consciousness where praxis is 'the most authentic center' of human self-actualisation in the world.[6] Weaving is likened to the practice of yoga involving the self-disciplining of the body for the fulfillment of goals in this world and the hereafter. To 'live prosperously' or *vaghya valamudan* is a popular Tamil adage used both as a blessing and a maxim of daily life by KGR and many members of his community. Popularised by Vethathiri Maharishi (himself a weaver from the Sengundar Mudaliar caste grouping) the message of well-being re-enchants daily life through the conscious practice of disciplining the mind and body. KGR and his family have invested both time and resources in promoting his teachings through SKY or 'simplified *kundalini* yoga' at the centre in Kumbakonam.

Summoning 'community' in handloom weaving, production and consumption as it has unfolded in this study does not mean nostalgia for artisanship as an exceptional category of human experience or a return to industry's archaic 'other' via craft. That handloom reform and revival has been a limiting development project is brought home in the professionalisation of 'craft' and the engagement of designers with artisans as labouring bodies. As agents of 'rescue and redemption,' designers only serve to reproduce 'the global hierarchy of value,' confining artisanal work within wider structures of power.[7] The imbrication of communities of practice within contemporary global regimes of design, development, heritage, trade, education and politics therefore is an emergent theme requiring further research.[8] For the moment, however, it is critical to have first exhumed shared work from state and non-state agendas and shed light on how it articulates community in all its discursive formations.

Imagining community as a process rather than a fixed vessel containing the accoutrements of identity is an invitation to conceive the 'work of community' as being regenerative. Rejecting the mind-body distinction inherent in the exoticised (and infantilised) image of the crafting ethnological 'body at work'[9] my aim has been to broaden the notion of artisanship and to rethink its many encumbrances. Participatory parity as artisan-citizens in formal arenas of education, commerce, politics and governance is denied to 'bearers of craft traditions,' who continue to seek support and recognition through different instruments and agencies of state dispensations. In fact their modernist location in the private domain of the household and hereditary caste stresses the interiority and indeed inferiority of their work. Viewing community for-itself rather in-itself therefore has been critical to the analysis of an artisanal subjectivity.

The Padma Saliyar claim of community as 'original' producers of the Kanchipuram sari is hinged on the narrativisation of a shared past, but the rights to patrimony embodying the assertion of 'tradition' are squarely rooted in the present. Heritage production and preservation involves economic, political and social stakes for individuals, groups and nations. Challenging dominant notions of 'culture' and viewing 'tradition' as a dialogic process of contestation and negotiation permits us to resist valuations of artisanal products on the basis of their alienation value or estrangement from the present.[10] In *We Who Wove*, handloom weaving and exchange comes to inhabit collective identity and purposefulness in all its human entanglements. Here livelihood practice, transformed

Fig. 7.1b: Cover of the *Padma Saliyar Kural*'s August 2017 issue felicitating India's new President Ram Nath Kovind and Vice-President Venkaiah Naidu. After the caste association was re-registered in 2016, the Sangam logo on the letterhead as well as the cover of the monthly now bears the number 108/2016. Additionally, images of Bhavanarishi and Bhadravathi appear on the left and that of Markandaya rishi on the right.

Source: Courtesy, Tamil Nadu Padma Saliyar Sangam, Chennai.

into a shared ethic and aesthetic of daily work, forms a renewed axis of difference in a substratum of competing legitimations.

I have grappled with the claims of community not to resolve questions of rupture, continuity and change in the long twentieth century but to mark milestones through the intimations of history with ethnography. In writing, narrating and historicising biographies of people, places and objects one has collided with epistemic hegemonies of caste, class, craft, nation and development. Going past spatialised identities I have sought to address a politics of differentiation from the vantage of the interstices—of mobile subject positions. But raising questions from the middle is neither a resolution nor a revision of minority histories. If discursive praxis is to hold any promise as a legitimate fulcrum of community-in-the-making then it must continue to invite interrogation of and opposition to hardened inequalities following the methodologies of radical feminist and Dalit politics.

We Who Wove, I hope, will resonate with all of us who are inspired by the words of African-American writer and liberative thinker James Baldwin, who said, 'You've got to tell the world how to treat you. If the world tells you how you are going to be treated, you are in trouble.'

ENDNOTES

1. I agree with Williams for whom 'consciousness is seen from the beginning as part of the human material social process, and its products in "ideas" are then as much part of this process as material products themselves' (1994 [2013]: 179).

2. This is similar to the work of Graeber (2006) in the anthropology of value.

3. Joseph 1998: 33.

4. In doing so I ascribe agential force to subaltern 'constructions of historicity' following the Subaltern Studies project of recovering 'minority histories and subaltern pasts' (Chakrabarty 1998).

5. Swaminathan 1992: 1611.

6. Praxis is 'the most authentic center' of human self-actualisation in the world (King 1991: 324).

7. DeNicola and DeNicola (2012) employ Herzfeld's (2004) 'global hierarchy of value' to explicate how designers have become agents of the devaluation of artisans' bodies and labour under contemporary global capitalist regimes.

8. See, for instance, a brief note on this position in Kawlra 2013.

9. cf. Mathur 2007.

10. Agamben has shown how the authenticity of an object derives from its 'alienation value' which has considerable economic significance (Agamben 1999 [1994]: 64–5).

BIBLIOGRAPHY

Agamben, G. 1999. *The Man without Content*. Originally published in Italian under the title *L'uomo senza Contenuto* by Quodlibet, 1994. Stanford: Stanford University Press.

Amalsad, D. M. 1925. *Handloom Industry in the Madras Presidency*. Madras: Government Press.

———. 1961. *Handloom Weaving*. Madras: Orient Longman.

Anandhi, S. 1991. 'Women's Question in the Dravidian Movement c. 1925–1948.' *Social Scientist* 19(5/6): 24–41.

———. 2005. 'Caste and Gender in Colonial South India.' *Economic and Political Weekly* 40(15): 1518–1522.

Ananth, S. 1991. 'The Institutions of the Vishwakarma.' *Architecture + Design*. September–October: 77–84.

Apffel-Marglin, F. 1985. *Wives of the God-King: The Rituals of the Devadasis of Puri*. Delhi and Oxford: Oxford University Press.

———. 1993. 'Women's Blood: Challenging the Discourse of Development.' *The Ecologist Asia* 1(2): 4–16. Bombay.

Appadurai, A. 1974. 'Right and Left-hand Castes in South India.' *Indian and Economic and Social History Review* 11(2): 216–259.

———. 1981. *Worship and Conflict Under Colonial Rule. A South Indian Case*. Cambridge: Cambridge University Press.

———. 1986. 'Introduction: Commodities and the Politics of Value.' In *The Social Life of Things: Commodities in Cultural Perspective*, ed. A. Appadurai. 3–63. Cambridge: Cambridge University Press.

Appadurai, A. 1995. 'Production of Locality.' In *Counterworks: Managing the Diversity of Knowledge*, ed. Richard Fardon. 204–225. Routledge.

Appadurai, A. and C. Breckenridge. 1976. 'The South Indian Temple: Authority, Honour and Redistribution.' *Contributions to Indian Sociology* 10(2): 187–211.

Arivukkarasi, N. A. and K. Nagaraj. 2009. 'Some Aspects of Socioeconomic Change in Rural Arani with Special Reference to Silk Weaving Industry.' Paper for the International Conference on *Market Town, Market Society, Informal Economy*. Contemporary South Asian Studies Programme. Oxford University, June.

Arterburn, Y. J. 1982. *The Loom of Interdependence: Silk Weaving Cooperatives in Kanchipuram*. Delhi: Hindustan Publishing Corporation.

Baker, C. J. 1981. 'Colonial Rule and the Internal Economy in Twentieth-Century Madras.' *Modern Asian Studies* 15(3): 575–602.

______. 1984. *An Indian Rural Economy, 1880–1955: The Tamilnadu Countryside*. Delhi: Oxford University Press.

Banerjee, M. and D. Miller. 2004. *The Sari*. New Delhi: Lustre Press/ Roli Books.

Banerjee, N. N. 1977. *Weaving Mechanism*. 6th edition. West Bengal: Tanimalaya.

Barnett, Stephen A. 1975. 'Approaches to Changes in Caste Ideology in South India.' In *Essays on South India*, ed. Burton Stein. *Asian Studies at Hawaii* 15: 64–91. Honolulu: University Press of Hawaii.

Basile, E. 2013. *Capitalist Development in India's Informal Economy*. London and New York: Routledge.

Bayly, C. A. 1988. *Indian Society and the Making of the British Empire*. Cambridge: Cambridge University Press.

Bayly, S. 2001. *Caste, Society and Politics in India from the Eighteenth Century to the Modern Age* Vol. 3. New York: Cambridge University Press.

Bharathan, K. 1985. 'The Living Art of Kancheepuram.' In *Frontline* 29 December–11 January: 94–102.

Beck, Brenda E. F. 1969. 'Colour and Heat in South Indian Ritual.' *Man* 4: 553–572.

______. 1972. *Peasant Society in Konku. A Study of Right and Left Subcastes in South India*. Vancouver: University of British Columbia Press.

______. 1973. 'The Right-left Division of South Indian Society.' In *Right and Left: Essays on Dual Symbolic Classification*, ed. Rodney Needham. Chicago: University of Chicago Press.

Beck, Brenda E. F. 1976. 'The Symbolic Merger of Body, Space, and Cosmos in Hindu Tamil Nadu.' *Contributions to Indian Sociology* n.s. 10(2): 213–243.

Boas, G. 1973. 'Macrocosm and Microcosm.' *Dictionary on the History of Ideas. Studies of Selected Pivotal Ideas.* Vol. III: 126–136. New York: Charles Scribner's Sons.

Bonazzoli, G. 2003. 'Puranic Spirituality.' In *Hindu Spirituality: Postclassical and Modern*, eds. K. R. Sundararajan and B. Mukerji. 159–185. Delhi: By arrangement with Crossword Publishing Company, USA.

Bourdieu, P. 1977. *Outline of a Theory of Practice* [Esquisse d'une Théorie de la Pratique, Précédé de Trois études d'ethnologie Kabyle, 1972], trans. Richard Nice. California: Stanford University Press.

Bradford, N. J. 1985. 'The Indian Renouncer: Structure and Transformation in a Lingayat Community.' In *Indian Religion*, eds. R. Burghart and A. Cantlie. London: Curzon Press.

Brennig, J. 1990. 'Textiles Producers and Production in Late Seventeenth Century Coromandel.' In *Merchants, Markets and the State in Early Modern India*, ed. S. Subrahmanyam. Delhi: IESHR and Oxford University Press.

Brimnes, N. 1999. *Constructing the Colonial Encounter: Right and Left Hand Castes in Early Colonial South India.* NIAS Monograph 81. London: Curzon Press.

Bythell, D. 1969. *The Handloom Weavers: A Study in the English Cotton Industry during the Industrial Revolution.* Cambridge: Cambridge University Press.

Bundgaard, H. 1999. *Indian Art Worlds in Contention: Local, Regional and National Discourses on Orissan Patta Paintings. Nordic Institute of Asian Studies* 80, and Curzon.

Carman, J. B. and F. A. Marglin, eds. 1985. *Purity and Auspiciousness in Indian Society*. Leiden: Brill.

Carroll, L. 1978. 'Colonial Perceptions of Indian Society and the Emergence of Caste(s) Associations.' *Journal of Asian Studies* 37(2): 233–250.

Census of India. 1961a. *Handlooms in Madras State*, IX, Part XI-A, ed. P. K. Nambiar. New Delhi: Government Publication, 1964.

______. 1961b. *Silk Weaving of Kanchipuram*, IX, Part VII-A. Handicraft Survey Monograph, No. 1, ed. P. K. Nambiar. New Delhi: Government Publication, 1964.

Chakrabarty. D. 1998. 'Minority Histories, Subaltern Pasts.' *Postcolonial Studies: Culture, Politics, Economy* 1(1):15–29.

Chari, S. 2004. *Fraternal Capital: Peasant-workers, Self-made Men, and Globalization in Provincial India*. New Delhi: Orient BlackSwan.

Charsley, S. R. 1982. *Culture and Sericulture. Social Anthropology in a South Indian Livestock Industry*. London: Academic Press.

Chatterjee, P. 1989. 'Caste and Subaltern Consciousness.' In *Subaltern Studies VI*, ed. R. Guha. Delhi: Oxford University Press.

______. 1998. 'Community in the East.' *Economic and Political Weekly* 33(6): 277–282.

Chatterton, A. 1912. *Industrial Evolution in India*. Madras: The Hindu Office.

Chennakrishnan, B. C. Salem. 1980. *Makarishi Markandeya Sarithai* [The Story of Markandeya Rishi]. Produced with the support of Nalli Subramaniam Chettiar, Nalli Design Centre, Kanchipuram, and Nalli Kuppuswami Chettiar, T. Nagar. Chennai: Tamil Nadu Padma Saliyar Sangam.

Chettiar, A. trans. 1905. *Bhavanarishi Puranam* (in Tamil) and overseen by Tamil scholar Subbarama Ayyar. Madurai: Native College. Second and third editions 1987 and 2010.

Ciotti, M. 2007. 'Ethnohistories Behind Local and Global Bazaars: Chronicle of a Chamar Weaving Community in the Banaras Region.' *Contributions to Indian Sociology* 41(3): 321–354.

Clothey, F. W. 1982. 'Chronometry, Cosmology and the Festival Calendar in the Murukan Cult.' In *Religious Festivals in South India and Sri Lanka*, eds. G. R. Welbon and G. E. Yocum. New Delhi: Manohar.

Coorlawala, U. A. 2004. 'The Sanskritized Body.' *Dance Research Journal*, 36(02): 50–63.

Coomaraswamy, A. K. 1909a. *Essays in National Idealism*. Madras: Ganesh Press. Reprint, New Delhi: Munshiram Manoharlal, 1981.

______. 1909b. *The Indian Craftsman*. With a Foreword by Alvin C. Moore Jr. Reprint, New Delhi: Munshiram Manoharlal, 1989.

______. 1911. *Art and Swadeshi*. Madras: Ganesh Press.

Dallapiccola, A. L. 2010. *South Indian Paintings: A Catalogue of the British Museum Collection*. Ahmedabad: Mapin Publishers.

Daniel, E. V. 1984. *Fluid Signs: Being a Person the Tamil Way*. California: University of California Press.

Das, R. K. 1964. *Temples of Tamilnadu*. Bombay: Bharatiya Vidya Bhavan.

Das, V. 1976. 'The Uses of Liminality: Society and Cosmos in Hinduism.' *Contributions to Indian Sociology* n.s. 10: 245–265.

Das, V. 1982. *Structure and Cognition: Aspects of Hindu Caste and Ritual.* Bombay: Oxford University Press.

______. 1985. 'Paradigms of Body Symbolism: An Analysis of Selected Themes in Hindu Culture.' *In Indian Religion*, eds. Richard Burghart and Audrey Cantlie. London: Curzon Press.

De Neve, G. 2005. 'Weaving for IKEA in South India: Subcontracting, Labour Markets and Gender Relations in a Global Value Chain.' In *Globalising India: Perspectives from Below*, eds. C. J. Fuller and J. Assayag. London: Anthem Press.

DeNicola, A. O. 2004. *Creating Borders, Maintaining Boundaries: Traditional Work and Global Markets in Bagru's Handblock Textile Industry.* Anthropology—Dissertations and Theses. Paper 34. http://surface.syr.edu/ant_etd/34

DeNicola, A. O. and L. DeNicola. 2012. 'Rescue and Redemption: Design Schools, Traditional Craft and the Nation-state in Contemporary India.' *Cultural Studies* 26(6): 787–813.

Department of Handlooms and Textiles, Government of Tamil Nadu. 2005. 'Kanchipuram Silks.' *Geographical Indications Journal of the Government of India* No. 4, 1 January, Application No. 15. Chennai: Intellectual Property of India, Geographical Indications Registry Chennai. http://ipindia.nic.in/girindia/

Dewan, D. 2004. 'The Body at Work: Colonial Art Education and the Figure of the Native Craftsman.' In *Confronting the Body: The Politics of Physicality in Colonial and Post-Colonial India*, eds. J. H. Mills and S. Sen. 118–133. London: Anthem Press.

Dickey, S. 1993. 'The Politics of Adulation: Cinema and the Production of Politicians in South India.' *Journal of Asian Studies* 52(2): 340–372.

Dilley, R. 1987. 'Myth and Meaning and the Tukolor Loom.' *Man* n.s. 22: 256–266.

Dirks, N. 1987. *The Hollow Crown: Ethno-history of an Indian Kingdom.* Cambridge: Cambridge University Press.

______. 1988. 'The Invention of Caste: Civil Society in Colonial India.' CRSO Working Paper 368 http://hdl.handle.net/2027.42/51136

______. 2001. *Castes of Mind: Colonialism and the Making of British India.* Princeton: Princeton University Press.

Douglas, M. 1970. *Natural Symbols: Exploration in Cosmology.* London: The Cresset Press.

______. 2004. 'Traditional Culture - Let's Hear No More about It.' In *Culture and Public Action*, eds. V. Rao and M. Walton. 85–109. California: World Bank and Stanford University Press.

Driver, F. and S. Ashmore. 2010. 'The Mobile Museum: Collecting and Circulating Indian Textiles in Victorian Britain.' *Victorian Studies* 52(3): 353–385.

Dumont, L. 1970. 'World Renunciation in Indian Religions.' In *Religion, Politics and History in India.* Collected Papers in Indian Sociology. Paris/The Hague: Mouton.

Egnor, M. T. 1983. 'Death and Nurturance in Indian Systems of Healing.' *Social Science and Medicine* 17(14): 935–945.

Fabian, J. 1983. *Time and the Other: How Anthropology Makes its Object.* New York: Columbia University Press.

Fontefrancesco, M. F. 2012. 'Crafting the Local: GIs, Jewelry, and Transformations in Valenza, Italy.' *Social Analysis* 56(3): 89–107.

Frasca, R. 1975. 'Weavers in Pre-Modern South India.' *Economic and Political Weekly* 10(30): 1119–1123.

Fraser, N. 1990. 'Rethinking the Public Sphere: A Contribution to the Critique of Actually Existing Democracy.' *Social Text* 25/26: 56–80.

Frost, M. R. 2011. 'That Great Ocean of Idealism: Calcutta, the Tagore Circle and the Idea of Asia (1900–1920).' Nalanda-Sriwijaya Centre, Working Paper Series No. 3. June. Singapore: Institute of Southeast Asian Studies in Singapore, http://nsc.iseas.edu.sg/documents/working_papers/nscwps003.pdf.

Fuller, C. J. 1984. *Servants of the Goddess: The Priests of a South Indian Temple.* Cambridge: Cambridge University Press.

Gamble, J. 2001. 'Modelling the Invisible: The Pedagogy of Craft Apprenticeship.' *Studies in Continuing Education* 23(2): 185–200.

Gandhi, M. K. 1921. 'Of Tamil Women.' In *The Collected Works of Mahatma Gandhi* Vol. 24. 22 July 1921–25 October 1921. Ahmedabad: Navajivan Trust.

______. 1925. 'To American Friends.' *Young India*, 17 September 1925. In *The Collected Works of Mahatma Gandhi* Vol. 32. 17 June 1925–24 September 1925. Ahmedabad: Navajivan Trust.

______. 1955. 'Bread Labour.' In *Ashram Observances in Action.* Ahmedabad: Navajivan Trust.

______. 1969. 'Speech at Saurashtra Club, Madura, September 29, 1927.' In *The Collected Works of Mahatma Gandhi* Vol. 35. September 1927–January 1928. The Publications Division GOI, Ahmedabad: Navajivan Trust.

Ganguly-Scrace, R. 2001. *Global Issues, Local Contexts: The Rabi Das of West Bengal.* New Delhi: Orient BlackSwan.

Geetha, V. and S. V. Rajadurai. 1998. *Towards a Non-Brahmin Millennium: From Iyothee Thass to Periyar*. Calcutta: Samya.

Ghurye, G. S. 1951. *Indian Costume*. Bombay: Popular Prakashan.

Gopalaswami, S. 1995. 'Nulum Nulum' (in Tamil). *Padma Saliyar Kural* 7(4): 15. Chennai: Tamil Nadu Padma Saliyar Sangam.

Goody, E. N., ed. 1982. *From Craft to Industry: The Ethnography of Prow-industrial Cloth Production*. Cambridge: Cambridge University Press.

Gorringe, H. 2010. 'The New Caste Headmen? Dalit Movement Leadership in Tamil Nadu.' In *Power and Influence in India: Bosses, Lords and Captains*, eds. P. Price and A. E. Ruud. 119–143. London: Routledge.

Graeber, D. 2006. 'Turning Modes of Production Inside Out or, Why Capitalism is a Transformation of Slavery.' *Critique of Anthropology* 26(1): 61–85.

Greenough, P. 1996. 'Nation, Economy, and Tradition Displayed: The Indian Crafts Museum, New Delhi.' In *Consuming Modernity*, ed. C. A. Breckenridge. Delhi: Oxford University Press.

Hall, S. 2000. 'Who needs "Identity"?' In *Identity: A Reader*, eds. P. du Gay, J. Evans and P. Redman. 15–30, 155.2. IDE: Sage Publications Inc.

Handler, R. and J. Linnekin. 1984. 'Tradition, Genuine or Spurious.' *The Journal of American Folklore* 97(385): 273–290.

Hardgrave, R. 1979. 'When Stars Displace the Gods: The Folk Culture of Cinema in Tamil Nadu.' In *Essays in the Political Sociology of South India*. New Delhi: Usha Publications.

Harriss, John. 2015. 'Privilege in Dispute: Economic and Political Change and Caste Relations in Tamil Nadu Early in the 21st Century.' Simons Papers in Security and Development, No. 44/2015. School for International Studies, Simon Fraser University, Vancouver. September.

Harvey, D. 2001. 'Globalization and the "spatial fix".' *Geographische Revue* 2: 23–30.

Havell, E. B. 1902. 'Hand-loom Weaving in India.' Lecture delivered before the Indian Industrial Association. Calcutta.

______. 1908. *Essays on Indian Art, Industry and Education*. Madras: G. A. Natesan.

______. 1912. *The Basis for Artistic and Industrial Revival in India*. Reprint, New Delhi: Usha Publications, 1986.

Haynes, D. 1986. 'The Dynamics of Continuity in Indian Domestic Industry: Jari Manufacture in Surat, 1900–47.' *Indian Economic and Social History Review* 23(2): 127–149.

Haynes, D. 2013. 'The Making of the Hyper-Industrial City in Western India: The Transformation of Artisanal Towns into Middle-Sized Urban Centres, 1930–1970.' *South Asia: Journal of South Asian Studies* 36(3): 336–353.

Haynes, D. and T. Roy. 1999. 'Conceiving Mobility: Weavers' Migrations in Pre-colonial and Colonial India.' *Indian Economic and Social History Review* 36(1): 35–67.

Haynes, D., A. McGowan, T. Roy and H. Yanagisawa. 2010. *Towards a History of Consumption in South Asia*. New Delhi: Oxford University Press India.

Herzfeld, M. 2004. *The Body Impolitic: Artisans and Artifice in the Global Hierarchy of Value*. Chicago: University of Chicago Press.

______. 2015. 'Common Sense, Anthropology of.' In *International Encyclopedia of the Social and Behavioral Sciences*, ed. James D. Wright. Vol. 4, 2nd edition. 258–262. Oxford: Elsevier.

Hobsbawm, E. J. 1984. 'Artisan or Labour Aristocrat?' *The Economic History Review* 37(3): 355–372.

Hubert, H. and M. Mauss. 1964. *Sacrifice: Its Nature and Function*, trans. D. Halls. Chicago: The University of Chicago Press. Midway Reprint, 1981.

Irschick, E. F. 1969. *Politics and Social Conflict in South India: The Non-Brahman Movement and Tamil Separatism, 1916–1929* (No. 3). Berkeley: University of California Press.

______. 1986. *Tamil Revivalism in the 1930s*. Madras: Cre-A Publishers.

______. 1994. *Dialogue and History: Constructing South India, 1795–1895*. Delhi: Oxford University Press.

Iyer, D. S. V. 1967. 'Looms.' *Marg* 15(4): 56–62.

Joseph, M. 1998. 'The Performance of Production and Consumption.' *Social Text* 54: 25–61. Spring.

Kalakshetra. 1985. *Brochure: Kalakshetra Golden Jubilee Art Festival*. Madras.

______. 1990. *Homage to Rukmini Devi: An Exhibition*. Catalogue of Exhibition co-sponsored by Co-ptex and Kalakshetra.

Kapur-Chishti, R., M. Singh and R. Jain. 2000. *Handcrafted Indian Textiles: Tradition and Beyond*. New Delhi: Lustre Press.

Katiyar, V. S. 2009. *Indian Saris: Traditions – Perspectives – Design*. New Delhi: Wisdom Tree.

Kawlra, A. 2002. 'The Kimono Body.' In *Fashion Theory: The Journal of Dress, Body and Culture*. Vol. 6, Issue 3. September. New York: FIT and UK: Berg Publishers.

______. 2005. 'Kanchipuram Sari: Design for Auspiciousness.' *Design Issues: Design in India* 21(4): 54–67. MIT Press.

Kawlra, A. 2013. 'Overwritten and/or Erased: Rereading Biographies of Cloth in the Global Ecumene.' Report on the ICAS 8 Macau Roundtable *Cloth, Identity and Power* in *The IIAS Newsletter* 65: 45. Leiden: The Netherlands. Autumn. http://www.iias.nl/the-newsletter/article/overwritten-andor-erased-rereading-biographies-cloth-global-ecumene

———. 2014. 'Duplicating the Local: GI and the Politics of "Place" in Kanchipuram, Tamil Nadu.' *NMML Occasional Paper*, Perspectives in Indian Development NS No. 29. New Delhi: Nehru Memorial Museum and Library.

Kemper, S. 1978. 'Time, Person and Gender in Sinhalese Astrology and Sinhalese Life.' Paper presented at the 1978 American Anthropological Association meetings, Los Angeles.

Kersenboom-Story, S. C. 1987. *Nityasumangali*. Chennai: Motilal Banarsidass.

King, I. T. 1991. 'Political Economy and the "Laws of Beauty": Aesthetics, Economics and Materialism in Marx.' *Science and Society* 55(3): 323–335.

Knorringa, P. 1999. 'Artisan Labour in the Agra Footwear Industry: Continued Informality and Changing Threats.' *Contributions to Indian Sociology* 33(1–2): 303–328.

Koppedrayer, K. I. 1991. 'Are Śūdras Entitled to Ride in the Palanquin?' *Contributions to Indian Sociology* 25(2): 191–210.

Kramrisch, S. 1959. 'Traditions of the Indian Craftsman.' In *Traditional India: Structure and Change*, ed. M. Singer. Philadelphia: The American Folklore Society.

Kumar, Nita. 1988. *The Artisans of Benaras: Popular Culture and Identity, 1880–1986*. Princeton: Princeton University Press.

Kumbakonam Handloom Silk Cloth Producer's Association. 1994. *Directory of Members 1994–95* (in Tamil). Kumbakonam.

Kuppuswami, N. 1983. *Work is Worship*. Madras: Arunothayam. New edition, 2004.

———. 1991. *How to Build Business*. Madras: Arunothayam.

Lave, J. and E. Wenger. 1991. *Situated Learning: Legitimate Peripheral Participation*. Cambridge: Cambridge University Press.

Levi-Strauss, C. 1963. 'Split Representation in the Art of Asia and America.' In *Structural Anthropology*, trans. C. Jacobson and B. G. Schoepf. Harmondsworth: Penguin Books.

Liebl, M. and T. Roy. 2003. 'Handmade in India: Preliminary Analysis of Crafts Producers and Crafts Production.' *Economic and Political Weekly* 38(51/52): 5366–5376.

Long, B. J. 1982. 'Mahasivaratri: The *Saiva* Festival of Repentance.' In *Religious Festivals in South India and Sri Lanka*, eds. G. R. Welbon and G. E. Yocum. Delhi: Manohar.

Ludden, D. 1993. 'Transformations of Colonial Knowledge.' In *Orientalism and the Postcolonial Predicament: Perspectives on South Asia*, eds. C. A. Breckenridge and Peter van der Veer. 250–278. Philadelphia: University of Pennsylvania Press.

———. 1996. 'Caste Society and Units of Production in Early Modern South India.' In *Institutions and Economic Change in South Asia*, eds. B. Stein and S. Subrahmanyam. Delhi. Oxford University Press and SOAS Studies in South Asia, Understandings and Perspectives Series.

Madan, T. N. 1991. 'Auspiciousness and Purity: Some Reconsiderations.' *Contributions to Indian Sociology* N.S. 25(2): 287–294.

Madras University. 1982. *Tamil Lexicon*. 6 Vols. Madras: Macmillan.

Mahalingam, T. V., ed. 1972. *Mackenzie Manuscripts: Summaries of the Historical Manuscripts in the Mackenzie Collection*. Vols. I and II. Madras: University of Madras.

Mahadevan, R. and M. Vijayabaskar. 2014. 'The Making of Non-Corporate Capital: Some Historical and Contemporary Entrepreneurial Narratives from Tiruppur, Tamil Nadu.' Nehru Memorial Museum and Library, Occasional Paper, Perspectives in Indian Development N. S. 33. New Delhi: NMML.

Mamidipudi, A., B. Syamasundari and W. Bijker. 2012. 'Mobilising Discourses: Handloom as Sustainable Socio-Technology.' *Economic and Political Weekly* 47(25): 41–51.

Marglin, S. A. 1990. 'Losing Touch: The Cultural Conditions of Worker Accommodation and Resistance.' In *Dominating Knowledge: Development, Culture and Resistance*, eds. F. Apffel-Marglin and S. Marglin. 217–282. Oxford: Clarendon Press.

Marchand, T. H. 2008. 'Muscles, Morals and Mind: Craft Apprenticeship and the Formation of Person.' *British Journal of Educational Studies* 56(3): 245–271.

Maskiell, M. 1999. 'Embroidering the Past: Phulkari Textiles and Gendered Work as "Tradition" and "Heritage" in Colonial and Contemporary Punjab.' *The Journal of Asian Studies* 58(02): 361–388.

———. 2002. 'Consuming Kashmir: Shawls and Empires, 1500–2000.' *Journal of World History* 13(1): 27–65.

Mathur, S. 2007. *India by Design: Colonial History and Cultural Display*. Berkeley, L.A. and London: University of California Press.

Mauss, M. 1973. 'Techniques of the Body.' *Economy and Society* 2(1): 70–88. First published in French in 1935.

McGowan, A. S. 2005. 'All that is Rare, Characteristic or Beautiful: Design and the Defense of Tradition in Colonial India, 1851–1903.' *Journal of Material Culture* 10(3): 263–287.

______. 2009. *Crafting the Nation in Colonial India*. US: Palgrave Macmillan.

Mehta, D. 1992. 'The Semiotics of Weaving: A Case Study.' *Contributions to Indian Sociology* n.s. 26(1): 77–114.

______. 1997. *Work, Ritual, Biography: A Muslim Community in North India*. Delhi: Oxford University Press.

Merrey, K. L. 1982. 'The Hindu Festival Calendar.' In *Religious Festivals in South India and Sri Lanka*, eds. G. R. Welbon and G. E. Yocum. Delhi: Manohar.

Messick, B. 1987. 'Subordinate Discourse: Women, Weaving, and Gender Relations in North Africa.' *American Ethnologist* 14(2): 210–225. May.

Metcalf, T. R. 1989. *An Imperial Vision. Indian Architecture and Britian's Raj*. London: Faber and Faber.

Michell, G. ed. 1993. *Temple Towns of Tamilnadu*. Bombay: Marg Publications.

Mines, M. 1984. *The Warrior Merchants: Textiles, Trade and Territory in South India*. Cambridge: Cambridge University Press.

Mines, M. and V. Gourishankar. 1990. 'Leadership and Individuality in South Asia: The Case of the South Indian Big-man.' *Journal of Asian Studies* 49: 761–786.

Miryam, K. D. W. 2014. 'Caste and Work: Weaving in Nineteenth-Century South India.' In *Towards a New History of Work*, ed. S. Bhattacharya. 97–120. New Delhi: Tulika Books and Association of Indian Labour Historian and V. V. Giri National Labour Institute.

Mitter, P. 1977. *Much Maligned Monsters: History of European Reactions to Indian Art*. Oxford: Oxford University Press.

Mohsini, M. 2011. 'Crafts, Artisans, and the Nation-State in India'. In *A Companion to the Anthropology of India*, ed. I. Clark-Deces. 186–201. Oxford, UK: Wiley-Blackwell.

Mosse, D. 2006. 'Collective Action, Common Property, and Social Capital in South India: An Anthropological Commentary.' *Economic Development and Cultural Change* 54(3): 695–724.

Nagaraj, K., S. Janakarajan, D. Jayaraj, and B. Harriss-White. 1996. 'Sociological Aspects of Silk Weaving in Arni and its Environs.' Unpublished paper. Chennai: Madras Institute of Development Studies.

Narayana Rao, D. 1925. *Report of the Survey of Cottage Industries in the Madras Presidency*. Government of Madras.

Narayanaswami Naidu, B. V. 1948. *Report on the Court of Enquiry into the Labour Conditions in the Handloom Industry*. Government of Madras.

Narayanaswami Pillai, T. M. 1955. *Report of the Committee on Cooperation in Madras*. Madras: Department of Industries.

Nevile, P. 1996. *Nautch Girls of India: Dancers, Singers, Playmates*. New Delhi: Ravi Kumar and Prakriti India.

Obeyesekere, G. 1976. 'The Impact of Ayurvedic Ideas on the Culture and the Individual in Sri Lanka.' In *Asian Medical Systems: A Comparative Study*, ed. C. Leslie. Berkeley: University of California Press.

Pandian, M. S. S. 1992. *The Image Trap: M. G. Ramachandran in Film and Politics*. New Delhi: Sage Publications.

______. 1993. 'Denationalising the Past: "Nation" in E. V. Ramasamy's Political Discourse.' *Economic and Political Weekly* 28(42): 2282–2287. http://www.jstor.org/stable/4400290

______. 1994. 'Notes on the Transformation of "Dravidian" Ideology: Tamilnadu, c. 1900–1940.' *Social Scientist* 22(5/6): 84–104. http://doi.org/10.2307/3517904

______. 1995. 'Beyond Colonial Crumbs: Cambridge School, Identity Politics and Dravidian Movement(s).' *Economic and Political Weekly* 30(7/8): 385–391.

______. 1996. 'Towards National-Popular: Notes on Self-Respecters' Tamil.' *Economic and Political Weekly*, 31(51): 3323–3329. http://www.jstor.org/stable/4404910

______. 2002. 'One Step Outside Modernity: Caste, Identity Politics and Public Sphere.' *Economic and Political Weekly* 37(18): 1735–1741.

Parthasarathi, P. 2001. *The Transition to a Colonial Economy: Weavers, Merchants and Kings in South India, 1720–1800*. Cambridge: Cambridge University Press.

Paxson, H. 2010. 'Locating Value in Artisan Cheese: Reverse Engineering *Terroir* for New-World Landscapes.' *American Anthropologist* 112(3): 444–457.

Prasad, S. C. 2001. 'Exploring Gandhian Science: A Case Study of the Khadi Movement.' Unpublished Ph.D. thesis, Dept. of Humanities and Social Science, IIT Delhi. Available at https://www.researchgate.net/publication/288737414_Exploring_Gandhian_Science_A_Case _study_of_the_Khadi_Movement

Price, P. G. 1991. 'Acting in Public versus Forming a Public: Conflict Processing and Political Mobilization in Nineteenth Century South India.' *South Asia: Journal of South Asian Studies* 14(1): 91–121.

———. 1996. *Kingship and Political Practice in Colonial India*. Cambridge: Cambridge University Press.

Purushottaman, K. R. 2005. 'Thirimbi Parkiren' [Looking Back]. In *Satabhishekha Malar* (in Tamil). 9–27. Chennai: Tamil Nadu Padma Saliyar Sangam, released on the occasion of the 70th birthday celebration of K. G. Ramaswami Chettiar of Kumbakonam.

Radhakrishnan, P. 1990. 'Backward Classes in Tamil Nadu: 1872–1988.' *Economic and Political Weekly* 25(10): 509–520.

———. 1993. 'Communal Representation in Tamil Nadu, 1850–1916. The Pre Non-Brahmin Movement Phase.' *Economic and Political Weekly* 27(31): 1585–1597.

Raheja, G. G. 1988. *The Poison in the Gift: Ritual, Prestation, and the Dominant Caste in a North Indian Village*. Chicago and London: University of Chicago Press.

———. 1996. 'Caste, Nationalism, and the Speech of the Colonized: Entextualization and Disciplinary Control in India.' *American Ethnologist* 23: 496–513.

Rajagopalachari, C. 1953. 'Education Through Work.' Text of speech delivered on 21 August, at Chingleput district in Tamil Nadu. Reprinted in *Rajaji's Speeches* II: 164–170. Bombay: Bhartiya Vidya Bhavan, 1978.

Ramani, S. 2002. *Sari: The Kalakshetra Tradition*. Craft Education and Research Centre. Chennai: Kalakshetra Foundation.

Ramakrishan, N. 2001. *The Dawn of the Weavers' Cooperative Movement* in Tamil. Kanchipuram: Sengai Mavatta Kai Thari Nesavu Thozhilalar Sangam.

Ramanaiah, M. V. (compilation) n.d. Evidence Vouchsafed by Goddess Padmavathi of Tiruchanur Given in Favour of the Padmasalis. Tirupati: Tirupati Padmsali Welfare Association. With the compliments of Tamilnadu Padmasali Association, Madras.

Ramaswamy, V. 1981. 'Weaver Folk Traditions as a Source of History.' *Indian Economic and Social History Review* 19(1): 47–62.

———. 1985a. *Textile and Weavers in Medieval South India*. Delhi: Oxford University Press.

———. 1985b. 'Artisans in Vijayanagar Society.' *Indian Economic and Social History Review* 22(4): 417–444.

Ranga, N. G. 1930. *The Economics of Handlooms*. Bombay: Taraporevala.

Rangarajan, M., N. Balakrishnan, and Deepa Bhatnagar eds. 2014. *Selected Works of C. Rajagopalachari* Vol. II, 1921–22. New Delhi: Nehru Memorial Museum and Library and Orient BlackSwan.

Reddy, D. and J. Zavos. 2009. 'Temple Publics: Religious Institutions and the Construction of Contemporary Hindu Communities.' *International Journal of Hindu Studies* 13(3): 241–260.

Reiniche, M-L. 1987. 'Worship of Kaliyamman in Some Tamil Villages: The Sacrifice of the Warrior-weavers.' In *Religion and Society in South India*, eds. V. Sundaram, G Prakash Reddy and M. Suryanarayana. Delhi: B. R. Publishing Corporation.

Report. 1908. *Proceedings of the Conference on All India Weaving Competition*, held at the School of Arts, Madras, on 2nd and 3rd March. Madras: Srinivasa Varadachari and Co.

Roy, T. 1993. *Artisans and Industrialization: Indian Weaving in the Twentieth Century*. Delhi: Oxford University Press.

———. 1997. 'Capitalism and Community: A Study of the Madurai Sourashtras.' *Indian Economic and Social History Review* 34(4): 437–463.

———. 1998. 'Development or Distortion? "Powerlooms" in India, 1950–1997.' *Economic and Political Weekly* 33(16): 897–911. 18 April.

———. 2000. 'De-industrialisation: Alternative View.' *Economic and Political Weekly* 35(17): 1442–1447.

———. 2002. 'Acceptance of Innovations in Early Twentieth-century Indian Weaving.' *The Economic History Review* 55(3): 507–532.

———. 2007. 'Out of Tradition: Master Artisans and Economic Change in Colonial India.' *The Journal of Asian Studies* 66(4): 963–991.

———. 2010. 'Consumption and Craftsmanship in India, 1870–1940.' In *Towards a History of Consumption in South Asia*, eds. D. Haynes, A. Mcgowan, T. Roy, and H. Yanagisawa. 268–297. New Delhi: Oxford University Press.

Rudner, D. W. 1987. 'Religious Gifting and Inland Commerce in Seventeenth Century South India.' *The Journal of Asian Studies* 46(2): 361–379.

Runkle, S. 2004. 'Making "Miss India": Constructing Gender, Power and the Nation.' *South Asian Popular Culture* 2(2): 145–159.

Schneider, J. 1987. 'The Anthropology of Cloth.' *Annual Review of Anthropology* 16: 409–448.

Scott. J. C. 1976. *The Moral Economy of the Peasant: Rebellion and Subsistence in South-east Asia*. New Haven and London: Yale University Press.

Scrase, T. J. 2003. 'Precarious Production: Globalisation and Artisan Labour in the Third World.' *Third World Quarterly* 24(3): 449–461.

Sen. A. 1987. 'Gender and Cooperative Conflicts.' In *Persistent Inequalities, Women and World Development*, ed. Irene Tinker. Economic and Social Commission for Asia and the Pacific. New York: United Nations.

Silverstein, M., and G. Urban. 1996. *Natural Histories of Discourse.* Chicago: University of Chicago Press.

Sinha, S. 1990. *The Development of Indian Silk: A Wealth of Opportunities.* London: Intermediate Technology Publications.

______. 2008. 'Lineages of the Developmentalist State: Transnationality and Village India, 1900–1965.' *Comparative Studies in Society and History* 50(01): 57–90.

Specker, K. 1989. 'Madras Handlooms in the Nineteenth Century.' *Indian Economic and Social History Review* 26(2): 131–166.

Srinivasan, A. 1985. 'Reform and Revival: The Devadasi and Her Dance.' *Economic and Political Weekly* 20(44): 1869–1876.

______. 1988. 'Reform or Continuity? Temple Prostitution and the Community in the Madras Presidency.' In *Structures of Patriarchy: State, Community and Household in Modernising Asia*, ed. Bina Agarwal. 175–198. London: Zed Books.

Srinivasan, P. 1983. 'The Sari Unwinds: South Indian Traditions, 1850–1983.' In *Pudu Pavu*. Exhibition Catalogue Madras: Co-optex.

Stein, B. 1968. 'Social Mobility and Medieval South Indian Sects.' In *Social Mobility in the Caste System in India: An Interdisciplinary Symposium*, ed. J. Silverberg. The Hague: Mouton.

______. 1977. 'Temples and Tamil Country.' *Indian Economic and Social History Review* 14(1): 11–46.

______. 1980. *Peasant State and Society in Medieval South India.* Delhi: Oxford University Press.

Stein, B., and S. Subrahmanyam, eds. 1996. *Institutions and Economic Change in South Asia.* Delhi: Oxford University Press. SOAS Studies on South Asia. Understandings and Perspectives Series.

Sthapati, G. V. 1978. *Shilpasshennul* (in Tamil). Madras: Thozil Mutpakku Kalvi lyakkam.

Subramanian, A. 2009. *Shorelines: Space and Rights in South India.* Stanford: Stanford University Press.

Sundar, P. 1995. *Patrons and Philistines: Arts and the State in British India, 1773–1947.* Oxford: Oxford University Press.

Swallow, D. 1982. 'Production and Control in the Indian Garment Export Industry.' In *From Craft to Industry: The Ethnography of*

Proto-industrial Cloth Production, ed. E. Goody. Cambridge: Cambridge University Press.

Swaminathan, P. 1992. 'Technical Education and Industrial Development in Madras Presidency: Illusions of a Policy in the Making.' *Economic and Political Weekly* 27(30): 1611–1622. 25 July.

Talavasek, O., and V. Svaty. 1981. *Shuttleless Weaving Mechanisms*. Textile Science and Technology 3. Amsterdam, Oxford, New York: Elsevier Scientific Publishing Co.

Tambiah, S. J. 1982. 'The Renouncer: His Individuality and his Community.' In *Way of Life: King, Householder, Renouncer Essays in Honour of Louis Dumont*, ed. T. N. Madan. New Delhi: IEG, Vikas Publishing House.

Tamil Nadu Padma Saliyar Sangam. 1993. *Virzha Malar* (in Tamil). Souvenir of Festival held on 1 August. Kumbakonam.

Tarapor, M. 1980. 'John Lockwood Kipling and British Art Education in India.' *Victorian Studies* 24(1): 53–81.

Tarar, N. O. 2011. 'From "Primitive" Artisans to "Modern" Craftsmen: Colonialism, Culture, and Art Education in the Late Nineteenth-century Punjab.' *South Asian Studies* 27(2): 199–219.

Thapar, R. 1982. 'The Householder and the Renouncer in the Brahmanical and Buddhist Traditions.' In *Way of Life: King, Householder, Renouncer Essays in Honour of Louis Dumont*, ed. T. N. Madan. New Delhi: IEG, Vikas Publishing House.

Thilakendran, C. 2005. 'Namadu Sangha Varalaru' [The History of Our Caste Association]. In *Satabhishekha Malar*. 37–46. Chennai: Tamil Nadu Padma Saliyar Sangam. Released on the occasion of the 70th birthday celebration of K. G. Ramaswami Chettiar of Kumbakonam.

Thompson, E. P. 1963. *The Making of the English Working Class*. New York: Pantheon.

Thurston, E. 1899. *Monograph on the Silk Fabric Industry of the Madras Presidency*. Madras: Government Museum.

Thurston, E., and K. Rangachari. 1909. *Castes and Tribes of Southern India*. 9 vols. Reprint. New Delhi: Asian Educational Services, 1987.

Uberoi, J. P. S. 2012. 'Marxism of Labour or Property?' *Economic and Political Weekly* 47(32): 73–80.

Ulin, R. C. 1996. *Vintages and Traditions: An Ethno-history of Southwest French Wine Cooperatives*. Washington D.C.: Smithsonian Institution Press.

______. 2002. 'Work as Cultural Production: Labour and Self-identity among South-West French Wine-Growers.' *Journal of the Royal Anthropological Institute* (n.s.) 8(4): 691–712.

Vatsyayana, K. 1983. *The Square and the Circle of the India Arts*. New Delhi: Abhinav.

Venkataraman, K. S. 1940. *The Handloom Industry in South India*. Madras: The Diocesan Press.

Venkatesan, S. 2009. *Craft Matters: Artisans, Development and the Indian Nation*. New Delhi and Hyderabad: Orient BlackSwan.

Visvanathan, S. 1985. *Organizing for Science: The Making of an Industrial Research Laboratory*. Delhi: Oxford University Press.

Wagoner, P. B. 2003. 'Pre-colonial Intellectuals and the Production of Colonial Knowledge.' *Comparative Studies in Society and History* 45(4): 783–814.

Walker, A. ed. 2009. *Tai Lands and Thailand: Community and State in Southeast Asia*. Honolulu: University of Hawaii Press.

Washbrook, D. 1997. 'From Comparative Sociology to Global History: Britain and India in the Pre-history of Modernity.' *Journal of the Economic and Social History of the Orient* 40(4): 410–443.

Wayman, A. 1982. 'The Human Body as Microcosm in India, Greek Cosmology, and Sixteenth Century Europe.' *History of Religions* 22(2): 172–190.

Weber, Max. 1948. *From Max Weber: Essays in Sociology*. Trans. and ed. H. H. Gerth and C. W. Mills. London: Routledge and Kegan Paul (paperback 1985).

Wilkinson-Weber, C. 2004. 'Women, Work and the Imagination of Craft in South Asia.' *Contemporary South Asia* 13(3): 287–306.

Williams, R. 1994 [2013]. 'Ideology.' In *Ideology*, edited and introduced by T. Eagleton. 175–189. London and New York: Routledge.

Wolf, E. R. 1982. *Europe and the People without History*. Berkeley: University of California Press.

———. 1984. 'Culture: Panacea or Problem?' *American Antiquity* 49(2): 393–400.

———. 1990. 'Facing Power – Old Insights, New Questions.' *American Anthropologist* 92: 586–596.

Yanagisawa, H. 1993. 'The Handloom Industry and its Market Structure: The Case of the Madras Presidency in the First Half of the Twentieth Century.' *Indian Economic and Social History Review* 30(1): 1–27.

Young, I. M. 1986. 'The Ideal of Community and the Politics of Difference.' *Social Theory and Practice* 12(1): 1–26.

Zimmerman, F. B. 1979. 'Remarks on the Body in Ayurvedic Medicine.' *South Asian Digest of Regional Writing* 18: 10–26.

Zimmerman, A. 1997. 'The Ideology of the Machine and the Spirit of the Factory: Remarx on Babbage and Ure.' *Cultural Critique* 37: 5–29.

APPENDIX

A district-wise list of Bhavanarishi shrines in Tamil Nadu
Courtesy: Tamil Nadu Padma Saliyar Sangam, Chennai

District	**Town/Village**
Chennai	Mandaveli; Old Washermenpettai
Kanchipuram	Narayanapalayam Street; Singhaperumalkoil Street
Villupuram	Siruvanthadu; Thirukoilur; Sandapettai
Cuddalore	Anguchettipalayam
Thiruchirapally	Ramjinagar; Allithurai; Pothavur; Kulumani; Kopu; Sennagarai; Magalampudur; Paithamparai; Mettupalayam; Kottapalayam; Vairichettipalayam; Kannanur; Kattanampatti; Kollathur; Eragudi; Puvalur; Puvalur Mathanam; Sankanthi; Samayapuram; Narasinghmangalam; Edumalai; Uyakondanthirumalai; Kattaputhur
Karur	Thogaimalai; Karur Town; Vengamedu; Koyampalli; Puliyur; Lalapettu; Kulithalai; Thanneerpalli; Uppidamangalam

Perampalur	Kurur; Sattiramanai; Veppanthattai
Ariyalur	T. Pallur; Karaipakkam
Kovai/Coimbatore	Edayarpalayam
Salem	Athur; Arasipalyam; Shevapettai; Salem town
Nammakal	Rasipuram
Dharampuri	Pennakaram; Hillarihalli
Dindigal	Vathalakunda; Palani; Ellandakottai; Nilakottai; Senpatti
Madurai	Avaniapuram; Chinthanai; Nadukottai; Vaadipatti; Munisalai; Melakottai
Theni	Sadapatti; Vatukapatti; Periyakulam
Sivagangai	Palaiayanur; Karaikudi
Thiruvarur	Mannarkudi; Valankaiman; Sooramangalam
Nagapattinam	Thinmalai Rayapattinam
Thanjavur	Aduthurai; Thirucherai; Thirumangalakudi; Kurichimalai; Thirunageswaran; Kumbakonam; Swamimalai; Kandiyur; Kadamabakudi; Kovilkudi
Vellore	Gudiyatham

INDEX